Technical Writing:

A Reference Guide to Reports, E-mails, Resumes, and More

Serena Henning

JP Publishing, LLC

Table of Contents

Summary

This book provides a comprehensive and simplified guide on how to improve your technical writing. The first part of this guide will go through the fundamentals of technical writing: what it involves, some of its central problems, how to establish yourself as a credible author, and how to approach your work. This is designed to assist all audiences in building the groundworks for technical writing, and to help shift common perceptions of its difficulties.

The rest of this guide will go into more detail about the specifics of different technical writing formats. This will go through the ins and outs of shorter and longer forms of technical writing, ranging from memos, to CVs, to reports and proposals. Each section will include a thorough overview of what the form of technical writing involves, things to do and to avoid, samples and exercises for you to try at home.

What is covered in this book:

- What is "technical writing"?
- What are the main problems inherent to technical writing?
- How to establish your voice.
- How to establish credibility.
- Useful language in technical writing.
- How to design your work.
- How to construct a piece.
- Assembling correspondence.
- Assembling CVs and resumes.
- Assembling short reports.
- Assembling long reports.

- Assembling proposals.
- Assembling summaries.
- Assembling user manuals.
- Web and blog writing.
- How to use graphics.

Introduction

Technical writing can be a daunting and oftentimes tedious process, whether you are a student, instructor, or office professional. From constructing a job resume, to sending an important client an email, to writing up a recommendation report, achieving the correct content and tone can seem like alien territory and leave the writer feeling frustrated and out of place.

This guide demonstrates how the intimidating parts of writing technically aren't actually all they are cracked up to be. Unlike many guides on this topic, which often overcomplicate technical writing, this book deploys a methodical, simplified, and rigorous approach so that the real difficulties in technical writing can be confronted and overcome.

Who is this guide for?

The simplified nature of this guide means that it is suitable for anyone hoping to improve on their technical writing. By nature, technical writing is used across a range of professions and sectors. This is different to academic writing, for example, which is clearly designed for the scholarly field.

Overall, this guide is designed to help:

- **Students**
The abundance of information on the Internet is overwhelming enough, let alone all the career and professional guidance available at university. This is by no means a bad thing, but when you're overworked and stretched for time, it can be difficult to scout out what is actually useful. This book brings together the

most important elements that you need to know about technical writing - whether it's applying for that first job or writing an email to your supervisor.

- **Office professionals**

The repetitive nature of office work can easily get you stuck in some bad habits, especially with regards to your writing. This guide is designed to get you out of your rut and refresh you on some of the key pointers of technical writing. Whether its revamping your memo style or improving on your "netiquette", this guide will have you covered.

- **Instructors**

Your work, in essence, is technical writing. It is essential, therefore, that you have an approach, and knowledge, to produce good quality work efficiently and effectively. By going through this step by step methodical guide, your working style will be reorganized and strengthened.

What is technical writing?

Before we start anything, however, we need to lay down the basics. What actually is technical writing? Simply put, to write technically is to communicate about a subject which requires instruction, explanation, or illustration. This is a distinctive type of writing that differs from other forms such as creative or academic writing. Stylistically, it is direct, clear, informative, and concise and usually written "objectively".

Although "technical writing" is often used to refer to writing which relates to science or engineering (i.e., technical subjects), this is not the definition adopted here. By "technical writing", we refer to different methods of written communication where the purpose of writing is predominantly informative.

Its Uses

One of the central characteristics of technical writing is that it is simple and easy to understand; a clear and efficient way of explaining a subject and how it works. This subject may be physically present or more abstract; something which can be seen or touched, such as when assembling a table, or something that is not directly present, such as a policy proposal.

Examples include:

- CVs/ resumes
- Proposals
- Memorandums
- A long report summary

The problems when writing technically

Communicating about communication?

"To attempt to communicate about communication is to be confronted at once with a peculiar epistemological paradox. The very subject we are to describe is used as a tool of the description. By doing so, we are somehow continuously forced to stand in our own shadow." (Merloo, 1967).

Have you ever been asked "What is communication?" before? In a classroom, or perhaps you've asked this question to yourself?

"Communication" is so overused as a buzzword that it often seems somehow void of meaning. This is in part because it is such a broad term, that encompasses so many different types of behaviors, from having a conversation with someone to watching TV, or witnessing non-verbal communication.

Worse, like Merloo points out in the quote above, you have to *use communication precisely to define what communication is..* All of these factors combined make defining "communication" a surprisingly difficult task and, actually, no one has a very satisfactory answer to the question "what is communication?".

The accepted definition is usually "the transmission of information", a definition which describes what communication does, rather than pinpoints what makes communication what it is. Essentially, this definition is comparable to answering the question "what is a table?" by pointing at a table. The best we can do is to describe or illustrate the concept.

Why does all of this matter, you might be wondering? Precisely because this guide focuses on different types of technical writing-- which all vary widely in nature. What they have in common is that they all are ways to *communicate* on various matters, for different purposes, and to distinct audiences. And to top it all, this book essentially does what Merloo describes: in other words, communicating about communication.

This guide's approach

Already we can see that technical writing, ironically, may not be that simple. Its varied applications mean that a number of considerations must be involved whenever the author is adapting to a new form. This guide recognizes and responds to these complexities.

In the first part of the book, we will go through the foundations of technical writing, dealing with how to establish yourself as a credible author. This will go through how to position your voice, write in an unbiased manner, and set your tone as a technical writer. The next chapter will go further, outlining how to design any form of technical writing. Next, we will start to go through the specifics - focusing on how to construct different forms of technical writing. Starting on the shorter end, chapter 3 will outline how to assemble correspondence, including emails and memos. Chapter 4 will then go through the ins and outs of job applications, explaining how to construct resumes and cover letters.

In Chapter 5 and 6, we will move onto larger bodies of work, first going through how to assemble short reports and then moving onto long reports. Chapter 7 will then focus on assembling proposals, chapter 8 on assembling summaries and chapter 9 on assembling user manuals. Finally, in the last chapters of this guide, we will move onto some of the all-important "how tos"; chapter 10 will focus on web writing and chapter 11 on graphics.

Chapter 1:
Establishing credibility

So, now we know that technical writing is about explaining, illustrating, or instructing on a particular subject, whether that's a policy recommendation or a kitchen appliance. But what does that mean in terms of your role as a writer? How does your voice differ from that of an academic or creative writer, for example?

It is important to remember that technical writing is, primarily, functional. Opposed to creative writing, or even academic writing, you may assume that the technical writing style is less chic style or complex. Functional writing, however, does not necessarily clash with style. Style has often been confused with pretension when it comes to writing, and overcomplicated and obscure vocabulary are sometimes mixed up with actually good writing.

Contemporary attitudes towards writing, however, increasingly privilege *clarity*. As Lester Faigley puts it (2011), "Too often long sentences reflect wandering thoughts that the writer did not bother to go back and sort out" (p. 154). The influence of "business-speak" in society has more or less shifted the consensual requirements of "good writing" towards clarity and conciseness (Lanham, 2006). This applies not only to technical writing but is an overarching societal attitude towards writing.

Whether privileging clarity over flourish in writing is a good or a bad thing is really a matter of opinion. Ornamental writing and clarity don't necessarily have to be at odds with one another, but it is clear that technical writing demands a certain utilitarian tone. Many people, however, forget that this is legitimately a *stylistic* requirement.

Really, style isn't about writing in only *one way* that is stylish-- there are many different valid styles. Style is about finding the appropriate tone for the purpose of your writing and using suitable language for your target audience. In this way, the stylistic requirements of technical writing are no lesser than those of any other type of writing. The list below details the most prominent stylistic requirements of technical writing.

Objectivity

Technical writing may seem like it doesn't leave much space for subjective involvement. But whatever you are writing, it's important to remember that you are an individual with a subjective perspective, opinions, tastes, preferences, and values.

"Does objectivity matter that much when I'm writing a professional email or a report?", you might be wondering. Well, it does. Imagine an employee is asked to write a report about the fish population in their local river. The said employee is a climate change denier and writes the report with no mention of how rising temperatures in the local area's river have caused a large proportion of fish to migrate further North. This omission obviously has a dramatic impact on the content of the report!

There are things you can do to strive for objectivity in your technical writing:

- **Present balanced views.** Reporting the full extent of nuanced positions on a matter ensures you are not oversimplifying your writing or supporting a biased stance. (Smyth, 1996)

- **Don't leave information out.** Even if part of the data doesn't confirm your position or is not coherent with the overall trend in the data, always include it. Leaving important information out only weakens your writing and makes it easily refutable.

- **Don't get too personal.** Using the passive tense and the third person is one way to avoid saying "I", and it might help you steer away from including anecdotal personal experiences, which do not actually help your writing.

- **Always support your claims with evidence.** Presenting supporting facts forces you to address other possible views and contrasting position, which overall helps you to avoid focusing on your personal stance.

- **Reference properly!** This advice is of course tied to evidence, which should always come from a reputable source. We'll elaborate more on citation and referencing later in this chapter.

Sound reasoning

Part of establishing credibility as a writer is expressing yourself coherently, demonstrating a grasp on sound reasoning. A sound argument is an argument which does not present any logical flaws-- i.e., an argument that does not contradict itself. This isn't always as easy as it seems!

Faulty arguments, which are often used as kinds of tricks to convince audiences, are called fallacies. Since the birth of rhetoric-- the art of persuasion-- fallacies have been used in the political and judicial arenas to mislead and divert audiences' attention. Other obvious places you might read or hear a lot of fallacies are the news, or in advertising. A study conducted by the argumentation scholar Walton (2010) suggests that the reason why we are susceptible to fallacious arguments is because our brains use "heuristics", mental shortcuts, which sometimes lead us to jump to conclusions. These mental shortcuts may hold beliefs such as "If it is an expert opinion, defer to it. If there is no reason to think it is false, accept it as true." (Walton, 2010, p.2).

Although these shortcuts can be helpful in decision-making situations, it's important to try and avoid falling prey to these argumentative pitfalls in your technical writing. Being aware of possible fallacies is already a big step towards avoiding repeating them yourself. Luckily for us, common types of fallacies have been well-documented and commented on! Here is a list of faulty arguments you want to avoid in your technical writing:

- ***Argumentum ad verecundiam*
  (Appeal to authority)**

Example:
"Many doctors and scientists believe that a bowl of Special K cereal for breakfast everyday provides all the essential nutrients needed for an average adult."

This argument is not fallacious, in the sense that it does not contain a logical contradiction. However, you can see how an argument which rests solely on an unknown number of mysterious sources' opinion is not very strong. The above argument really *is* fallacious in the sense that sources are not named (and for all we know, they could be made up!). Another version of this type of fallacy is to present as evidence a claim by someone who is not an authority or expert on a matter (E.g. My friend Rebecca believes that a bowl of Special K cereal for breakfast everyday provides all the essential nutrients needed for an average adult).

- **Slippery slope**

A slippery slope argument infers a chain of negative consequences from a single premise. Because of the escalation in the negative consequences, the aim of a slippery slope argument is to demonstrate that the premise should be rejected.

Example (Stanford Encyclopedia of Philosophy, 2020):

> "You have decided not to go to college;
> If you don't go to college, you won't get a degree;
> If you don't get a degree, you won't get a good job;
> If you don't get a good job, you won't be able to enjoy life;
> But you should be able to enjoy life;
> So, you should go to college."

Enoch (2001) argues that slippery slope arguments often turn against themselves; although some slippery slope arguments may not always be entirely fallacious, distinguishing between valid inferences and invalid ones is a tricky business. It's a lot easier to avoid slippery slopes altogether!

- **_Argumentum ad hominem_**
  (argument against the person)

The ad hominem fallacy designates portraying your argumentative opponent negatively, in order to dismiss their point. By attacking "ad hominem" (Latin for "the person"), you target the arguer, rather than their actual stance.
Example:

"Ms. Clark's position on juvenile delinquency should be ignored, since she was herself arrested for public intoxication as a teenager."

This argument attacks the figure of Ms. Clark rather than her actual position on juvenile delinquency-- which might be a very interesting stance! Another way to use the ad hominem fallacy (Stanford Encyclopedia of Philosophy, 2020) is to suggest that the arguer is defending their position out of self-interest, or that the arguer does not follow their own stance. These are all strategies to discredit the argumentative opponent.

- **_Post hoc ergo propter hoc_**
  (after this, therefore because of this)

This type of fallacy infers causation from temporal succession; in other words, this form of argument establishes causality between two events which occurred in succession. It is a version of "because event 2 occurred after event 1, event 1 caused event 2."

Example:
"In country X, unemployment decreased in June, because the government reduced the payroll tax in January."

Just because event 2 (decrease of unemployment) happened after event 1 (government reduced payroll tax), it cannot be soundly inferred that event 1 caused event 2. There could be many other causes for the falling rates in unemployment.

- *Peititio principii*
  (begging the question):

This type of fallacy is also called a circular argument. It's a form of argument where the premise is logically equivalent to the conclusion; in other words, it's the logical equivalent to a dog chasing after its own tail.

The Stanford Encyclopedia of Philosophy cites Whately's (1875 III §13) example:

> "to allow everyman an unbounded freedom of speech must always be, on the whole, advantageous to the State; for it is highly conducive to the interest of the Community, that each individual should enjoy a liberty perfectly unlimited, of expressing his sentiments."

As you can see, this sentence is completely tautological (it repeats itself). Whately doesn't demonstrate anything, but only repeats his premise as the conclusion of his argument.

- **Straw man argument**

The straw man argument is a variation of the fallacy known as *ignoratio elenchi,* or irrelevant conclusion. Essentially, this consists in building a "straw man" of the opponent arguer's claim, distorting and simplifying their stance, in order to refute it more easily.

Arguer 1: Veganism could help reduce carbon emissions.
Arguer 2 (straw man): Veganism could solve all of the world's problems.

Because the straw man version of the argument is easy to refute (it's easy to prove that veganism wouldn't solve *every* problem across the planet), arguer 2 creates the impression that arguer 1's position is ludicrous and untenable.

The bottom line

All these Latin names and technical terms may seem like a lot but knowing these fallacies can help you avoid recreating them in your own writing!

Referencing

While you might think of referencing as the boring to-do chore at the bottom of your list, it is actually extremely important. Similar to using argumentative devices properly, referencing is a big part of being an intellectually honest writer. By citing precisely and accurately, you are essentially crediting other people for their hard work.

If you write on a laptop, using referencing software is a huge help. When you are writing, it's easy to lose track of your sources of information...which always leaves you in a kerfuffle at the very last minute, when you are trying to clean up your piece. Referencing software-systems you can easily download on your PC or MAC include:

- Zotero
- EndNote
- RefWorks
- Mendeley
- Citationsy

By using some of this software, you can keep track of your sources as you go along writing. However, whether you are entering references manually or with software, knowing common citation styles is important.

The lists below demonstrates the use of the APA citation system:

Referencing Books

1. Singular author:

Anderson, B. (1993). *Imagined communities: Reflections on the origins and spread of nationalism*. London, UK: Verso.

2. Multiple authors:

Greig, A., Taylor, J., & MacKay, T. (2013*). Doing research with children: A practical guide*. London: Sage.

3. Edition other than the first:

Buglear, J. (2010). *Stats mean business* (2nd ed.).
    Burlington, MA: Butterworth-Heinemann.

4. Chapter in a book:

Van de Vijver, F., & Leung, K. (2011). Equivalence and bias: A
    review of concepts, models, and data analytic procedures. In
    D. Matsumoto & F. Van de Vijver (Eds.), *Cross-cultural
    research methods in psychology* (pp. 17 - 45). Cambridge:
    Cambridge University Press.

5. Translated Book:

Castro, F. (2008). *My life* (A. Hurley, Trans.).
    New York, NY: Dover. (Original work published 2006).

6. Edited Book:

Belsey, C. (2006). Poststructuralism. In S. Malpas & P.Wake (Eds.),
    The Routledge companion to critical theory (pp. 51–61).
    New York, NY: Routledge.

Referencing journal articles

1. Online article DOI provided

Spitz, D., & Hunter, S. (2005). Contested codes: The social
    construction of Napster. *Information Society* 21(3), 169-180.
    doi:10.1080/01972240490951890

2. Print article (or no DOI)

Cuddy, C. (2002). Demystifying APA Style.
  Orthopaedic Nursing, 21(5), 35-42.

Referencing newspaper articles

1. Newspaper article

Rosenberg, G. (1997, March 31). Electronic discovery proves
  an effective legal weapon. *The New York Times*.
  Retrieved from http://www.nytimes.com.

2. Newspaper article with no author

Gulf News. Barcelona to ban burqa in municipal buildings.
  (2010, June 14). Retrieved from http://gulfnews.com.

For different sources (blogs, reports, archives etc.), always consult a citation guide. Quality guides are available online, such as WAC Clearinghouse's (2020).

Avoiding the waffle

Key to technical writing is making sense to as many people as possible. Have you ever come across an instruction manual that goes on a tangent about the historical origins of the screwdriver? Or an email that finishes with "thanking you kindly and gratefully this morning"? The answer, hopefully, is no.

Technical writing avoids the waffle and is defined by the widespread use of plain language. Unlike academic or creative writing, the use of plain language in technical writing seeks to make a point as clearly and concisely as possible. It helps avoid confusion and misunderstandings among its readership.

What is plain language?

Professor Robert Eagleson (Anastasia, 2020), an expert in modern English language, describes plain language as displaying the following characteristics:

- **Clarity**: the most understandable words are used in the shortest amount of space possible.
- **Message-focused:** the topic should take pride of place and should not be distracted through language.
- **Unpretentious**: obscure words and convoluted sentences are a no-no.
- **Professional**: simple language should be used, but it should be appropriate - no uses of slang or "baby talk".

How to write using plain language

Owing to its simple nature, there is a fairly straightforward way of using plain language. As mentioned, forms of technical writing vary widely, and a more extensive guide on how to write in different formats will come in the later sections of this book. However, there are some key basics which can provide you with a good foundation to begin with (Anastasia, 2020):

1. Important messages come at the beginning.
2. Convey one message in one sentence - no need for repetition.
3. Sentences should be short (typically no more than 25 words).
4. Use paragraphs - separate sections by an idea.

5. Short words are better. Why use "demonstration" when you could use "show"?
6. Avoid jargon. Check if necessary and remove or replace.
7. Use the active, rather than passive, voice; you pick up the apple - not the apple was picked up by you.

Exercises

1. Read the following sentences and rewrite them using plain language.
   - Because there is a need to reschedule the meeting that is being held later today, I am letting you know via email earlier so that you don't show up.
   - The large bar chart that is situated above this sentence is showing an increasingly large reduction in the amount of young people in all of the separate states in America buying housing properties.

2. You want to argue against a temporary ban on veganism put forward by a leading political figure, who argues that "it is bad for the economy". How would you go about this?

3. Create APA references for the following books.
   - The Bell Jar, by Sylvia Plath, published on 1971 by Harper & Row in New York, USA.
   - Nineteen Eighty-Four, by George Orwell, published on 8th June 1949 by Secker & Warburg in London, UK.
   - Harry Potter and The Philosopher's Stone, by J.K. Rowling, published on 26th June 1997 by Bloomsbury Publishing in London, UK.
   - The Great Gatsby, by F. Scott Fitzgerald, published on April 10th 1925 by Scribner in New York, USA.

- NW, by Zadie Smith, published, published on 27th August 2012 by Penguin in London, UK.

NOTES

Chapter 2:
Designing Your Work

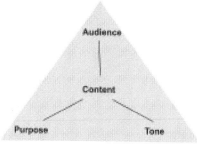

Now you know how to establish yourself as a writer, the next step is how to establish your work. This is the part of technical writing where you work out the whats, whys, whos and hows. For example, you will need to adapt your email if you are writing to a politic figure versus an academic.

A useful way of thinking about the design of your work is the Audience, Purpose, Tone, Content triangle (Lumen, 2020). Think of the audience, purpose, and tone of your work as integral to shaping the content that your produce.

These key steps to establishing the design of your work are outlined in the next sections.

Outlining your purpose

The first thing when writing anything is to outline your purpose; the reason that you are writing a piece. Works without a focus do not translate well to an audience. Why am I writing this piece and what do I hope to achieve? What is the purpose of my piece?

Here are some starter questions to get some of your technical juices flowing (Naas, 2020):

- What are you trying to do with your piece? Inform? Persuade? Instruct?
- How many purposes do you have and how many can you manage? If your text needs to be brief, you may need to cut down what you are trying to convey.

Identifying your audience

Another important question to ask when approaching technical writing is "who am I writing for?". This is the audience of your piece - the individual or group that you are intending to address (Lumen, 2020). A policy recommendation, for example, will most likely be geared towards those in the political sphere. Differently, an instruction manual on how to train a cat should be aimed at as wide an audience as possible.

It is essential, therefore, that you conduct an audience analysis before constructing your piece. An audience analysis involves the following considerations (Lumen, 2020):

- **Demographics**

This covers the core identity aspects about an audience - the data that would often be used to measure them. This may include age, gender, ethnicity, religious beliefs, class, or ability. Demographics will be important depending on how targeted your work is.

- **Existing knowledge**

It is also important to think about what your audience already knows. For example, writing a proposal to your manager will not require you to outline all of your existing qualifications – something which they hopefully already know!

- **Expectations**

What will your audience expect from your piece? Is there a general structure and layout to what you are writing? Think about appearance conventions, such as proper grammar and spelling, font type and font size.

- **Education**

Finally, education can also be an important factor when considering your target audience. For example, if you are writing correspondence with someone trained at a doctorate level, you may want to opt for more formal language than if you are writing to someone still completing their undergraduate degree.

One way to visualize your audience is to imagine writing your piece as giving a presentation. If you were giving training on public speaking to a corporate office, you would probably opt to wear conventional suit attire. Differently, if you were giving this training to a hip start-up, you might opt to whack out the Converse.

Finding the right tone

The way that you write is very much a reflection of your purpose and audience; it is the attitude that you are conveying towards a subject (Lumen, 2020). In everyday language, we use a variety of tones to communicate how we feel - conveyed through pitch, timing and what we are actually saying. All of this comes fairly intuitively but can be slightly more difficult to get across in writing.

There are a number of ways that you can set and adjust your tone in technical writing. Though technical communication is typically factual and serious, tone does vary when writing technically (ACS, 2020). For example, a non-profit annual report may go for a lighter tone than a CV. Here are some devices that you can adjust your tone:

- Sentence structure
- Word choice
- Punctuation
- Formal/ informal language
- Pace (influenced by the length of paragraphs, and use of lists and graphics)

Constructing your piece

Now that you have a basic idea of how to design your technical writing, it is important to have an understanding of how you are going to write it. There are a number of general stages that should be followed when constructing a piece of work, which will ensure that your piece is well-researched and rigorous. Though this may not be applicable to shorter forms of technical writing, these stages may be useful to think about. Here are the distinct steps when writing:

1. Prewriting
This is the part of the writing process that doesn't actually writing your piece. It is when you organize your ideas and build the foundations of your work. Prewriting is essentially the stage where you lay out your ideas and develop a sound reasoning to them. Strategies include:

- Listing: Generate a list of broad ideas and then reduce these down to smaller lists (University of Kansas, 2019). This is particularly useful when you need to narrow down your topic. You should try to thematically arrange your lists and then label groups of ideas which come together. In technical writing, you should also focus on your purpose, tone, and audience as central topic areas.

- Mind mapping: This is when you begin to infer the relationship between different groups of ideas. From your list, you should have some central subjects or themes emerge. Put these in the center of a page and write new ideas around the center, linking these with lines.

- Free writing: write non-stop for a certain amount of time to generate ideas. This allows you to develop your ideas on a topic without second-guessing yourself. Try to free write for around 5 or 10 minutes on a particular topic and then look over what you have written, highlighting the most prominent and interesting ideas.

2. Drafting

When drafting your piece, you are beginning to develop more cohesive work. Here you will begin to sketch out your ideas in writing. Don't worry about your spelling, grammar, or organization at this stage - these bits will be ironed out later!

3. Editing

This is the first stage of improving your draft - where you will identify some of the major errors or faults in reasoning. Identify the biggest problems in your work and make the necessary adjustments.

4. Redrafting

So, we're editing again? Didn't I just do that? There is a subtle difference between editing and redrafting. Whilst editing involves finding and fixing specific errors, redrafting is editing on a more fundamental level. This involves taking a step back and reviewing the cohesion of your entire piece. At this point, you may want to move around important parts or integrate an introduction or conclusion if you haven't already. Re-drafting often involves an entire re-write of the original piece and doing so will ultimately result in a higher quality piece of work.

5. Proofreading

Unlike redrafting, proofreading focusses on surface level errors such as spelling, grammar and referencing. This is the final stage in writing and should be done only when all other editing revisions have been made.

Exercises

1. You are creating an instruction guide on how to look after your cat whilst you are away on holiday. This has been written for your long-term friend. What are the key aspects (demographic, education, expectations, existing knowledge) of this audience that you should consider?

2. Same again, but this time you are writing a report on why Pitbulls should be legalized in your country which will be sent to leading political figures. What are the key aspects of this audience that you should consider?

3. Without looking, what are the key steps that should be followed when constructing a piece?

NOTES

Chapter 3:
Assembling Correspondence

What is correspondence?

Correspondence is the shortest form of technical writing, which may include emails, memos, text messages and letters. In today's climate of communication, these forms of written correspondence are usually transmitted online. This has led to the rise of "netiquette" - the codes of online-speak in a professional context.

"Netiquette"

The way that you communicate in writing carries a lot of significance. Virtual writing requires tact, skill and awareness and can often lead to someone obsessively re-reading their email and waiting a long time before pressing send (Last, 2020). This anxiety is understandable: unlike verbal communication, the Internet acts as an online archive of our communications, that could resurface in many years to come.

When corresponding online, therefore, you will want to represent yourself and/or your organization as best as possible, by deploying "netiquette" (Last, 2020). Communication should be clear and concise at a minimum. As with any form of technical writing, your content should always be determined by PAT: Purpose, Audience and Tone.

Emails

Emailing is familiar to almost everyone, from service users to students, having largely replaced print letters in everyday forms of correspondence. They are best used for brief messages but contain more content than a typical text message. Additionally, they vary in formality - ranging from the use of personal messages to business communication. This is an important thing to remember in emails; though they may seem like a fairly informal medium, appropriate respect should still be used in professional contexts (Last, 2020).

Here are some guidelines for constructing an email:

- **Appropriate salutations.** When addressing people externally, you should usually opt for "Dear" in your introductory email. If they are internal to your organization and you have a relationship with them, a simple "Hi" should suffice.

- **Be brief.** Try not to repeat yourself or include unnecessary information in your email.

- **Format properly.** An email should not be condensed into one block of text. Make sure to paragraph appropriately - usually in three or less.

- **Keep your subject line simple.** A cardinal sin in email correspondence is writing a waffly subject line; this immediately signals that something may be off with your communication skills. Choose the most relevant and brief summary of your email contents for your subject.

- **Sign off with a signature.** A signature block containing your name and key contact information will add a professional touch to your email.

- **This is not Facebook messenger.** No LMAO, ROFL or LOLs here please.

- **Review.** Make sure to check for spelling and grammatical mistakes - especially your recipients name. Also make sure to test that all attachments/ links are working and correct.

- **Don't leave people hanging.** Try to respond to an email within 24 hours. Likewise, if you don't receive a response to an important matter within a similar time frame, send a polite follow up.

Examples:

The following is an example of a poorly written email:

> Jan! I was thinking earlier that it would be rly fun to go to the climate conference on Saturday!!!! I've been thinking about it for agessss and think it will be really good. Don't leave me hanging LOL - Steph xx

The following is an improved version of the above:

Hi Jan,

Hope you're doing well. I was wondering if you would like to attend the climate conference on Saturday with me? I've heard that it's going to include some really interesting panels.

Look forward to hearing from you!

Kind regards,

Steph

Steph McLuskin
www.stephmcluskinstudios.co.uk
stephmcluskin@mcluskinstudios.org
+8887433672910

Useful language: emails

	Formal	Informal
Salutations:	Dear, To Whom It May Concern, (check appropriateness)	Hi,
Signoffs:	Yours sincerely, Kind regards, Best wishes,	Best, Regards, Thanks,

Texts

Though most often used amongst close friends, communicating via text is increasingly deployed in formal workplace settings.

The instinctively personal feeling of a text makes it even more essential that we think before we send. Once again, the PAT format should be followed when constructing a text. Additionally, you may want to be conscious of:

- **Misinterpretation**

Because of the brief nature of texting, and the use of symbols and other signs, your message may convey something that you did not intend. Make sure to re-read your text to check that it won't be taken the wrong way!

- **Borderline harassment**

Unlike emailing, texting can feel more invasive and needy. Only opt for texts when appropriate!

Basic memos

Unlike the above, memoranda or memos are specifically used to correspond "in-house"; they are a note, or a document usually sent from one person to one or more people in an organization. Though they are mostly informative, they can also be persuasive documents. Memos are commonly used to (Last, 2020):
- Pass on/ request information
- Outline policies
- Present short reports
- Propose ideas

The format of a memo is more complicated than an email, and many companies or organizations typically have their own styles or templates that are used. Overall, the main components of a memo are:

- **A logo or letterhead**

This is optional, but you may choose to include your organization's letterhead at the top of your memo (often in the righthand corner). This will include the company logo and sometimes the name, address and contact information.

- **A header block**

This will usually appear at the top left side of a memo, underneath the word **MEMO** or **MEMORANDUM** (in bold and caps). This is section which contains important information about the recipient, sender, and the subject of the memo. It will be formatted as follows:

TO: Recipients full name and their position within the organization (if applicable).
FROM: Sender's full name and their position within the organization.
DATE: The date of sending the memo.
SUBJECT: A short summary of the message contents.

- **The message**

This will vary in length depending on the subject matter of your memo; it may be a few sentences or a comprehensive report. Despite this, you should generally arrange the message of your memo like this:

1. **Opening:** Does your reader need to look at this and why?

2. **Details:** What does your reader need to know? This should include the main bulk of information and fulfil the central aims of your memo. You should not include unnecessary information here.

3. **Closing:** What should your reader do now? This may be the action, if there is any, that your reader is expected to take in

response. You should aim to be polite and outline how taking this action may benefit them.

It is important to remember that memos, like most forms of technical writing, are very concise; there is no need to provide a warm-up to your piece with a lengthy introduction. Because they are used in the workplace, they tend to be even more dry and direct. Also remember to use a readable font such as Arial or Times New Roman, in size 10-point or 12-point. The following is an example of a typical short office memo:

KUMA KITCHENS

Memorandum

TO: Felicity Chan, Director of Digital Marketing
FROM: Zoe Paris, Food Developer
DATE: April 22nd, 2020
SUBJECT: Christmas Photography

Due to the addition of future holidays to our issues, I wanted to inform you that we will need to move the scheduled date of Christmas photography from September 19th to July 5th.

The food testing department has agreed that, given the importance of the Christmas holiday as a major source of revenue for our magazine, the date for producing content should be shifted back. This has been approved by the Editor in Chief and will be provisionally implemented for this year.

I want to thank you in advance for your understanding and hope this will not cause too much disruption to your timetable. I would greatly appreciate it if you could send an updated agenda as soon as possible.

Useful language: memos

Opening: "I've noticed that", "Due to", "I'm writing to inform you that", "After speaking with".

Closing: "Thank you in advance for", "I am excited to discuss", "I look forward to", "We are confident that".

Exercises

1. You're writing an email to the director of a company that you're hoping to sell offices supplies to. How would you open and close your email?
2. What is the key information that should be included at the top of a memorandum?

NOTES

_____

_____

_____

_____

_____

Chapter 4:
Applying for Jobs

Job applications are stressful. The process of filling in application forms, rewriting your resume, and coming up with a solid cover letter is difficult enough by itself; on top of that, a concomitant rejection can be a tough blow to take. Of course, the more optimistic perspective is that job applications constitute an important step towards finding the right career path for you. Getting there, however, can be difficult at the best of times. The struggle to pin down an ideal job, for example, is often framed as a failure on the applicant's part. Many job searchers may experience depression (New York Times, 2019) when they do not find a job shortly after starting their search, accompanied by a sense of shame and defeat.

It's important to remember, then, that struggling to find work is hardly due to personal failure, but to an increasingly competitive job market. The growing use of application tracking systems has complicated job searching for applicants (Forbes, 2015), as many potentially well-suited candidates can be eliminated through keyword-tracking software.

Additionally, levels of higher education among populations continues to increase every year in the United States and in many countries around the world. The U.S. Census Bureau recently recorded the highest ever number of education levels among Americans: more than one third (33.4%) of the adult population in the U.S. held a bachelor's degree or higher in 2016 (U.S Census Bureau, 2017).

These factors, therefore, have created an unprecedented competitive climate in job markets. The average number of applications for any given job in the U.S. is 118 (Forbes, 2013), and for corporate employment, goes up to 250 (Glassdoor, 2015) per single job.

Although these figures may seem like a pretty dreary picture for jobseekers, remember, they also serve as a reassurance: increasing competitiveness for jobs does not mean that you are less valuable as a candidate. Rather, it has created a climate where learning to highlight your skills effectively is all the more important.

Ultimately, you should always remind yourself of the golden rule of job hunting: rejection is not a reflection of your abilities, but due to the lack of compatibility between applicant and hirer. Finding the *right* job isn't just about being able to do the tasks, it's about being comfortable in your workspace, believing in the values of your organization, and sharing the sensibility of your co-workers. If you don't get hired that one time, it's not because you couldn't do the job, it's because you and that particular job were probably incompatible in the first place.

Before you start applying

Before you start your job hunt, it is useful to identify and list your skills. This is a good base for your cover letter, which will have to go beyond listing your achievements. A cover letter (more on this later) should articulate your accomplishments in relation to the job that you are applying for, highlighting commonalities in the nature of the work or its objectives.

First, list the skills required by the job in one column. Then, try and relate a past achievement or experience to this. Your table could look something like this:

Skills required for the job...	Your experiences demonstrating these skills...
• Communication • Written communication • Verbal communication & listening	• Writing essays, writing for a student newspaper, writing reports • Making presentations, oral reports, teaching
• Leadership • Delegating tasks	• Endeavors you have started, membership to student club, or committees, etc.
• Managing workload	• Balancing two part-time jobs, or job and studying.
• Listening to others • Teamwork • Supporting others	• Mentoring program, tutoring. • Volunteering projects • Being a member of any team (club, society, etc).
• Setting up shared goals	• Delivering a project on tight deadline
• Organizing • Prioritizing	• Organizing an event
• Dealing with pressure • Time management	• University coursework or schoolwork or experience at other job
• IT skills • Using the Internet, email, calendar	• Experience using social

applications	media for a project
• Familiarity with software packages	• Demonstrated use of Microsoft, Outlook etc.

CVs and Resumes

What are CVs and Resumes?

Curriculum vitæ, Latin for the "course of one's life", commonly referred to as "CVs" by the Brits... you've probably guessed, we're talking about resumes. Whatever you might call them, resumes or CVs are anxiety-inducing. Simply put, CVs are a written summary of your skills, education, and work experience. They are essential to pretty much any job search and are often the difference in whether you are considered for a role.

Stressing over how to best convey your career profile in such a dry and drab document is a challenge, but the following chapter will help you get started on writing a solid version of your resume!

Layout and design

The most difficult part about writing a CV is often just taking the first step. Where do you start? And on top of that, the crippling fear of having nothing to write down on that page doesn't make things any easier. The best approach to getting over the initial fear is to try and come up with a basic skeleton of your education and work experience, which you can build on later for each new job application.

The basic sections in a CV are:

1. Education
2. Work experience
3. Additional experience
4. Languages and other skills
5. Interests/Awards

Non-academic CVs usually run over one or two pages (academic CVs are usually longer and provide details about publications, conferences etc.). Whether you choose to format your CV on one or two pages should depend on the details in the job description. A shorter one-page CV should simply be a more condensed version of the longer one-- this may force you to keep only the most relevant information on your resume!

How to organize each section

Each section (education, work experience etc.) can be broken down either in a chronological or a skills-based manner. A chronological structure, perhaps the most common, means your most recent experience will be featured at the top of each section, and the least recent one at the bottom. A skills-based structure is used only when the applicant has years of experience working in the same sector as the job applied for.

What not to include

- **Pictures**. Not of your dog, not of your graduation ceremony, and not even an ID pic! According to Graduateland.com, 80% of US employers will not consider your resume if it includes a profile photo. Although it depends on the country where you are applying, it's a rule of thumb that you should usually not include a picture of yourself, as hiring decisions are not meant to be made under the influence of gender, ethnicity, or appearance (though these can sometimes be inferred from your other information, such as your name).

- **Your nationality.** There is no need to specify your nationality on your resume unless it is explicitly requested by the job description.

- **Different colors**. Just stick to black and white paper. Although it might seem boring, it does look more professional and it is always a safe choice.

- **Eccentric fonts**. You want to stand out, but you don't want to stand out for the wrong reasons! The point is to draw the hiring manager's attention with your achievements and suitability for the position, not your brilliant display of varied font use. Stick to Arial or Times New Roman in a font between 10 and 12.

The "I have no experience" anxiety

Many things can count as experience on a resume. Just because you haven't had done an internship at J.P. Morgan doesn't mean you haven't done anything valuable. If you're worrying about a lack of experience to include on your resume, keep in mind the following:

- A big part of starting a new job is learning! Employers don't expect you to know everything already.

- You can demonstrate your skills and competences through other kinds of experiences than full-time positions or internships. Unpaid voluntary work can also testify to your skills and personality, as well as any kind of entrepreneurial, organizational endeavors!

- If you're applying for your first job, remember everyone has to start somewhere. It's O.K. to be starting out-- just keep that in mind when you are searching for jobs. Try and aim for entry-level positions which don't require previous experience.

Tailoring to the job

Once you have a standard resume listing all of your achievements, you will have to sort through the most relevant elements, and perhaps get rid of the less relevant ones, based on each position you are applying for. You shouldn't send out the exact same resume for each job application but try your best to personalize it each time. Although this might seem like a big waste of time, it does significantly increase your chances of catching the hiring manager's attention. It's certainly a better strategy to send out 5 personalized CV for 5 different positions than one standard CV to 10 different positions.

How to ensure relevance:

- **Choose your words carefully.** Read the job description closely-- the job ad asks the question "can you do this job?", and your resume and cover letter should be the answer to that question. So, it makes sense to pick up on key words in the job description and include them in your resume.

- **Make a checklist of all the criteria for the job**. Make sure you have illustrated each requested competency with something on your CV. This will show you are already paying attention to the requirements of the job, and that you are well-suited to the role.

- **Check out the organization's website.** Try and figure out who they are and what they're looking for: this can help you find the right words to resonate with the organization's message. This is a way to try to speak their language.

- **Present information in a positive light, but don't exaggerate!** Use active verbs like "organized" or "achieved" and steer away from derogatory or vague vocabulary. Don't overemphasize your past roles, however, otherwise this will probably show during an interview.

- **Use spell check and always formulate short, straightforward sentences.** A resume especially has no space for rambling! Aside from showing your brilliant synthesis skills, simple sentences just make it easier for the hiring manager to read your resume. Resumes can be quite cramped, so short sentences just save everybody involved from a migraine.

The heading

The heading of your resume should contain your name and contact information, usually presented in the following manner:

Jane Doe

j.doe@gmail.com | LinkedIn page or address | (555) 555-1234

You can include a professional email if you have one, or your university email if you haven't graduated yet. Otherwise, just use a personal email which you consult regularly.	You can include a blog or personal site if relevant; otherwise, you can optionally include your address.	An updated phone number with the appropriate area code, and which you use on a day-to-day basis

Example - The following page displays a standard CV example. You will most likely want to adapt this to your own preferences, but the layout and format of this template is a certainly a good place to start!

NOTES

_____

_____

_____

_____

_____

_____

_____

_____

Jane Doe

j.doe@gmail.com | Linkedin.com/JaneDoe | (555) 555-1234

Education

B.A., English
2014-2018
University of Toronto, Canada.

- 3.8 GPA

SAT Reasoning Text
2010-2014
Western Michigan High School

- 1500 SAT score
- Class valedictorian

Work Experience

Part-time Editorial Assistant Canadian Literature journal (Toronto)
February 2019 - Ongoing

- Provided editorial support to editor in chief (issuing contracts, dealing with royalties.
- Liaised with printing and photography services.
- In charge of a wide range of administrative duties, including phone and email queries.
- Assisted with special event reporting, such as conferences and special issues.

Internship at Nelson Education Ltd. Publishing House. (Toronto)
September 2018 – December 2018

- Proofreading, checking content, correcting grammatical, spelling and punctuation errors in manuscripts.
- Promoted books.

Additional experience

Shop Assistant at Barnes and Noble (Lansing, Michigan)

- Communicated with customers to ensure quality customer service.
- Managed book orders and deliveries.

Languages & IT

- English: Native speaker.
- Spanish: Native Speaker.
- French: fluent.
- Expert knowledge of Microsoft Word, Outlook and Excel.

Awards & Interests

- Advanced French studies diploma level C22, 2013.
- Member of the University of Toronto Track Team. 2014-2018.

Cover letters

How to write a cover letter

So, you've found the job you would like to apply for, tailored your resume to the job description, and now you're staring at a blank page, wishing for something to appear? Welcome to writing cover letters!

The initial skill-listing step should have helped you think about what you can bring to the organization and how you can highlight your relevant experiences. Articulating these into a well-written piece is what comes next. First, it's important to know the basic characteristics of a successful cover letter:

- **Brevity**. Unless explicitly specified, a cover letter should not be longer than one A4 page, or about 400 words. Short sentences, which do not exceed 14 words (LSE Careers, 2020) are preferable, and the style should be sharp and logical.

- **Formal greetings.** As a form of business correspondence, cover letters should always use a formal tone. This means cover letters usually begin with "Dear [Title and Last Name]". It is always best to know who will read your letter so that you can name them, and to end with "Your sincerely". If you do not know who to address the letter to, you may use "Dear Sir/Madam" or "Dear Hiring Manager", and end with "Yours faithfully".

- **Positive and enthusiastic language**. Use the active voice rather than the passive (i.e., "I created" as opposed to "was created") and include action words, such as "accomplish" and "undertake".

Cover letters should also include:

- **Your name and contact information** (phone number, email, and address) in the right-hand corner. It's also customary to include the organization's address on the left.

- **A logical structure.** How exactly you structure your letter is up to you, as there is no set formula for cover letters. Essentially, what matters is that it makes sense. One way to structure your letter is to divide it into two "why this job" and "why you" paragraphs (The University of Oxford Careers Service, 2020).

- **Correct spelling and grammar**. As usual, always use spell check when writing your cover letter, and make sure that you proofread it several times. Grammatical and spelling mistakes create a negative impression-- to be extra safe, get someone else to double check your letter if you can.

- **Relevant facts about the organization**. Show that you actually want to work there by including facts that you have researched. This shows that you are committed, and familiar with the organization's profile and values.

Demonstrating relevance
Remember, getting a job is all about *compatibility*; the main concern is to ensure that your cover letter portrays you as well-suited to the role. The obvious thing *not to do* is to write a generic, nondescript cover letter and send it to multiple organizations. Every cover letter you send should be a unique response to a specific job advertisement.
Furthermore, your cover letter shouldn't simply repeat the information on your resume: its purpose is to clearly state why

you are drawn to the position, and what value you can bring to the role.

A straightforward way of applying this advice is to use the STAR method. This approach ensures that your cover letter develops your experience in a relevant manner and is not superficially listed. STAR stands for Situation, Task, Action, Result: it provides a framework through which to detail your past experience (University of Oxford, 2020).

The spirit of the STAR approach is the idea of detailing experience, rather than shoving a multitude of loosely related achievements into your cover letter.

- Situation: Describe the *situation* you were in
- Task: clearly outline the *task* you had to accomplish
- Action: Elaborate on the *actions* you took
- Results: What *results* came out of this experience?

Example:

Superficial achievement description:
As the editor of The Red Panda Times, I undertook several projects to broaden our readership and develop the newspaper's online presence.

Improved STAR method:
As the editor for my college newspaper, *The Red Panda Times*, I was in charge of sourcing innovative content and ensuring the representation of the university's varied student body in *The Red Panda*'s publications. I considerably developed the newspaper's online presence and organized a monthly outreach event to recruit contributors and increase circulation. This resulted in a 25% increase in readership of *The Red Panda Times*, and in the addition of fifteen new regular contributors to our team.

Structuring a cover letter (Yale University, 2020).

1. Paragraph 1/ Why this job? Getting the reader's attention
- State who you are and why you are writing.
- Draw in the reader by providing a reason why you are interested in the role.
- Include information about the organization that you have gathered through research. This is a way to prove you know the organization and serves as evidence of your genuine interest in it.

The point of the first paragraph is to get your audience to keep reading. Catch their attention by using compelling reasons and language and try to think about what might resonate with them.

2. Paragraph 2/ Why you?
- Evidence how you are suited to this position by drawing links between the required skills and your past experience.
- Without repeating your resumé, focus on one or two achievements related to the tasks of the role.
- Detail one or two examples, using the STAR method, which demonstrate how your profile fits with the organization's culture and objectives.

This paragraph should constitute the argumentative chunk of your letter. Here, you should focus on providing evidence and supporting your case with one or two detailed examples, rather than a long list of unrelated accomplishments.

3. Paragraph 3/ Conclusion
- Reemphasize your interest in the position.
- Briefly wrap up your letter with a summary of why you are a good fit for this job.
- End the letter by thanking the reader for their time and consideration.

The last paragraph should effectively summarize what you can bring to the company or organization, and end on a positive note.

Example: The following is a sample cover letter

Darlene Simson

333 High Street

Kansas City, MO 34175

(111) 304-2222

d.simson@gmail.com

June 26, 2019

Hiring Manager

39 West Press

123 Summer Lane

Kansas City, MO 35467

Dear Ms. Blake,

I am writing to express my strong interest in the new editor position at 39 West Press. My combination of experience in freelance journalism and editing has made me an excellent fit for this role.

I am particularly drawn to this position because of 39 West Press' unique and inspiring publishing profile. I have always been a passionate writer, in fiction as well as nonfiction. Producing quality critical discourse on socio-political matters was the main focus of my college newspaper. This objective is evidently upheld by 39 West Press' publications, alongside a constant preoccupation with artistic and literary value. Your recent publication of the book of poems, *It's a Woman's World* (2019) demonstrates your commitment to promoting a diverse range of experiences and voices. This publishing culture echoes my own priorities as a writer and editor.

Having worked as an editor, an editorial assistant, and a freelance journalist, I am highly familiar with the full range of typical editorial duties. Producing quality writing on a tight deadline was the cornerstone of my freelancing job. As an editorial assistant for *The Kansas City Star*, I perfected my research and fact-checking sills. Finally, as the editor in chief for my college newspaper, I focused on shifting the editorial line to a more progressive and critical style. By organizing monthly outreach events and distributing the newspaper throughout various societies and clubs at the university, I succeeded in considerably diversifying our contributors' profiles and our overall content. My initiative resulted in the inclusion of a poem and art section, and a 15% increase in readership.

In light of my editing and writing experience, I believe I am an excellent fit for the editor role at 39 West Press. I am committed to broaden the world of publishing to include a wider variety of voices and would be honored to be a part of your editorial team. Thank you for your time and consideration, and please feel free to contact me for any further information.

Yours sincerely,

Darlene Simson

Useful language (London School of Economics, 2020)

Leadership
• coordinated • implemented • established • managed • led • directed • supervised • delegated • coached • allocated

Research
• analyzed • investigated • determined • experimented • surveyed • solved • synthesized

Communication
• trained • negotiated • influenced • consulted • presented • persuaded • interacted • advised • addressed

Organization

• streamlined • scheduled • encouraged • expanded • resolved • budgeted • (re)organized • prepared • administered

Interpersonal:

• collaborated • facilitated • mediated • consulted • liaised

Taking initiative:

• initiated • created • designed • established • launched • set up • conceived • implemented

Achievements:

• promoted • launched • developed • redefined • simplified • persevered • enhanced

• accelerated • improved • completed • produced • secured • increased • doubled

Exercises

1. What information should be included at the top of a CV?

2. You're applying for a waiting job at a Japanese restaurant. Thinking about the experience that you currently have, what would you include on your CV?

3. Use the appropriate language to make these selling points more CV ready.

   • I absolutely adore bees and plants and I have an allotment of my own with a beehive so I think that I would be a really good addition to your garden center.

   • I also used to work two jobs at once so I'm really good at doing loads of things all at once. I actually worked at a plant shop in the week and then on the weekends I did my neighbors gardening so I'm really knowledgeable about gardening.

4. Read the job description below. What are the top 3 skills you should highlight in your cover letter?

Title: Donations Officer

Role: To plan, develop and implement donations campaigns to Charity X, and expand the existing portfolio of potential donors.

Duties:

- Solicit donors, including public figures, able to make contributions and appearances to support Charity X' cause.
- Develop strategies to meet annual revenue goals.
- Maintain positive relations with contributors.
- Reach out to volunteers and liaise with the volunteering department.

5. Compare the following cover letter paragraphs. What are their strengths and weaknesses? Which would you say is more effective?

a.   To whom it may concern,

I am writing because I want to apply to the Donations Officer position at Charity X. I created a donation campaign for the charity group ABC at university, so the Donations Officer role should suit me well. I also want to continue working in fundraising, to keep improving my skills.

Here is what I have accomplished as student leader of the MSF donation campaign:

- *Exceeded donation goals*
- *Expanded the donor and contributor base*
- *Recruited dozens of new volunteers*
- *Organized ABC days at the university to raise awareness*

b.   Dear Hiring Manager,

It is my pleasure to apply to the Donations Officer position at Charity X. My considerable experience in the charity sector, combined with my dedication to your cause, position me as very well-suited to this role.

As the donation's leader for the charity group ABC, I have significantly developed my communication and leadership skills, as well as my ability to build lasting positive relationships with donors. By organizing monthly outreach events across my campus and the surrounding town, I succeeded in dramatically broadening ABC's donor portfolio. This resulted in a 3% excess in donation goals and the addition of twenty new volunteers to the donations program.

Notes

Chapter 5:
Assembling Short Reports

75% of engineers', business executives', and government officials' time is spent writing reports and letters or processing them (Mohan; Sharma, 2016, p. 213). This statistic speaks for itself: reading and writing business communications is one of the main tasks in many important decision-making professions.

Simply put, a report is an organized piece of writing which accounts for the facts of a situation, evaluates their significance, and formulates recommendations. The word report is from the Latin *"re-portare"*, literally to "carry back". Reports, therefore, are pieces of writing intended to "take the audience back" to past events for which the said audience was not present. Memorandums, meeting minutes, progress reports, or expense reports all qualify as reports, as they all document past occurrences.

On the surface "reports" may seem like quite a broad category -- it isn't that obvious what the commonality between a lab report and an expense report might be. Whether they are intended for an internal or external audience, whether their tone is informal or formal, or whether they are addressed upwards of the organization's hierarchy or downwards, reports may be divided into a wide variety of possible subcategories.

A very straightforward criterion used to separate different types of reports, however, is simply their length. In fact, length is often an indicator of other varying report characteristics, such as the degree of formality they require, and the nature of their purpose.

Broadly speaking, shorter reports tend to be more informal and informational, while longer reports are often formal and analytical. This chapter deals with short reports, which are often an extension of shorter forms of correspondence, and so follow on quite naturally from the previous section.

What is a short report?

Obviously, the central difference between a long and a short report lies in the length of the communication. But as mentioned above, beyond the brevity of its expression, a short report usually doesn't include conclusions or opinions by the author (ProPapers, 2020); it is descriptive or informational, rather than analytical. Conversely, the main purpose of longer reports is usually to provide a recommendation, which entails analyzing data and detailing the author's conclusions at length.

The following sections will outline different types of short reports and how to write them. These are memo reports, meeting minutes, progress reports, and expense reports, all widely used across different sectors.

Memo Reports

What is a memo report?

Although memorandums are often swapped for email today, memo reports are still used in many workplaces, so it is useful to know how to write one. Chapter 3 has already detailed the ins and outs of constructing basic in-house memos: a memo report takes this basic style and adapts it to a report format.

Somewhat differently to a basic memo, a memo report is usually written to provide information in response to a previous request. Its key purpose is to convey information regarding a decision or matter to an audience internal to the organization. Another difference compared to basic memos is that memo reports can sometimes include different sections, separated by headings, and may also include a reference list (Anderson, 2013).

How to write a memo report

It is important to remember that your report should not be no longer than two pages. The essential information which must be provided in a memo remains the same as in a basic memo: the receiver, the sender, the reference, the date, and the subject. Memo reports are usually divided into two sections:

1. The heading

The name of the organization is usually featured at the top of the memo, in the center. Underneath, information about the sender and the receiver should be included, as well as the reference and date. This will take a similar form to the basic memo (refer back to Chapter 3 for a more detailed explanation). Finally, the subject should be explicitly written right above the body of the memo.

KUMA KITCHENS

Interoffice memorandum

TO: Head of Sanitation and Hygiene Department

DATE: 23rd March 2019

FROM: Director of Human Resources

REFERENCE: W769 09

SUBJECT: **Upcoming food safety inspection**

---

2. The body

Although the contents of the body of a memo report are very different to that of a basic memo, the language used should be equally concise and straightforward. The body of a memo report can sometimes include (Anderson, 2013):

a. Opening

State the central purpose of the memo; why you are writing this report. This could include a statement of a problem which is being responded to. Keep this section short - up to two or three sentences should suffice.

b. Findings/ Recommendations/ Summary

Include this section (whichever heading works best for your piece) if your report is longer than a page. Provide a short statement outlining the main recommendations or findings in your report.

c. Discussion

This is the longest section of your memo, which will outline all of the evidence that you have collected to support your central findings. You should open with the most relevant information and separate out your discussion with subheadings:

d. Methods

Here you will briefly outline your approach to this report. For example, if this is a policy recommendation, you may have deployed quantitative or qualitative methodologies. If this is a report on a scientific experiment, you may wish to include information such as your setup and procedure.

e. Results

Describe the results of your research. This may be presented in words, but you can also include a table or graph.

f. Analysis

Briefly include an analysis of your findings. You don't need to provide lengthy paragraphs-- a short overview is appropriate for a memo report.

g. Commentary

If this section is included, it should expand on your analysis - what do your findings suggest? Implications, challenges, limitations, and further areas of research can be discussed.

h. Closing

You've made your point, and now it's time to summarize it. What action would you like for your reader to now take? Much like in a basic memo, you should make your request polite and succinct.

i. References

If you have cited material that is not your own in your report, provide references here (see Chapter 1 for more tips on how to reference).

j. Attachments

Attach anything that you couldn't include in your report. This may be additional information on your methodology, more detailed results, or further analysis. Unlike the rest of your report, there is no limit on what to include here. Make sure to give each attachment a heading.

Meeting Minutes

What are meeting minutes?
Meeting minutes are fairly straightforward: they are the documentation of meetings used to inform attendees and non-attendees about what was discussed (Heathfield, 2019). In brief, minutes are used to keep track of what happened during a meeting, and to facilitate the transition from discussion to action

During a meeting, a designated minutes taker is assigned the task of conducting the notetaking, typically on an electronic device. Meeting minutes may be distributed to all participants as soon as they have been checked over and approved by the meeting Chair. This may be right at the end of a meeting or within the following 24 hours. You may wish to use software to create and share your meeting minutes. Useful tools include Google Docs and One Note.

Keeping minutes is important, as they advise participants on their commitments and upcoming deadlines. They should transform the wealth of information in a meeting into manageable key points, without overwhelming the reader. Meeting minutes should always contain (Heathfield, 2019):
- A record of attendance (names of all participants).
- The decisions, commitments, and main points of discussion.
- The action items and deadlines that participants have signed up to.

The most important thing to note about minutes is that they are not intended to be perfect transcripts of everything said during the meeting. A note taker shouldn't be a *verbatim* stenographer, but rather, someone with good synthesis sills. Only the most relevant points in the meeting should be featured, and details about participants' interactions, such as emotions and feelings, are not to be included.

Additionally, keep in mind that minutes are a legal document which establish an organization's record of activity - it is even more essential then that professional and unbiased language is used (Oliver, 2020).

How to write meeting minutes

Today, there are lots of easily accessible meeting minutes templates available on most office software packages. However, it is still important to have a basic understanding of this administrative staple, which many workplaces will expect you to know. Meeting minutes should generally be organized as follows (Personify, 2020):

Organization Name
Meeting Minutes
Date

Opening
When, where the meeting was held and who called it to order.

Present
All members who were present.

Absent
Any members who were not present.

Approval of Agenda
Approval of Minutes

Business from the Previous Meeting
Motions or subjects that were raised previously, a short description, whether they

---

were approved or rejected.

New Business
Motions or subjects raised for the first time, a short description, whether they were approved or rejected.

Additions to the Agenda
Additional items raised by members.

Adjournment
What time the meeting was adjourned, by whom, and when and where the next meeting will be held.

Minutes submitted by: Name
Minutes approved by: Name

Expense Reports

What is an expense report?

Expense reports are an entirely different type of document: they are a much more circumscribed form of communication, written by an employee and addressed solely to the employer. Their purpose is to record expenditures made by an employee while on the job, for which the employee seeks reimbursement. Such expenses are documented, in order to keep track of the organization's spending and taxable profit. Although writing an expense report may seem like a chore, keeping track of who paid for what is essential to guarantee protection of employee rights. If you are an employee, you should take your expense reporting seriously-- it will certainly play in your favor in the long run!

From the company's side, expense reports are a fundamental part of closely monitoring spending. In some cases, they may help establish the need for the company to redistribute resources or to limit the expenditures budget allocated to employees. In fact, according to the expense managing software ExpensePoint, "studies have found that expense report fraud alone can cost companies up to 5% of their annual revenue". So, as an employee, recording your expenses while on the job will definitely put you in your boss' good books. And as an employer, rigorously monitoring expense reports by employees may save your company from expense report fraud!

What should be on your report:
- Your name and your contact information.
- A list of the purchases to be reimbursed featuring the date of each purchase.
- Description of the purchase (why was it bought? For whom?).
- A total of the amount of money spent.
- A subtraction of any advances (money given to you in advance for a business expenditure) you may have received
- The total sum of money to be reimbursed.

Some business expense reports may require more detail or space for more information. For example, a business trip over several days might require you to break the expenses down into more categories. For this kind of report, it's best to create more sections and provide further detail, such as:
- Accommodation
- Transportation
- Food
- Supplies, etc.

Each day may need to be broken down into the above section examples, to ensure that the expenses are rigorously recorded and justified. This also helps to prove that the expenses you made on a trip were for business and not pleasure.

Date	Description	Accommodation	Transport	Meals	Supplies	Other	Total

Subtotal

Advances

Total

Company Name / Logo
Purpose of expense report:
Name:
Contact information:

Progress reports

What is a progress report?
Intuitively, a progress report is a written record of what has already been completed and what is left to do on a project. There are a number of uses to a progress report, such as reassurance that progress is being made, formalizing the commitments and duties of team members, and to discuss potential issues in a project and its timescale (Boyd, 2020).

Progress reports can be used to evaluate the advancement of many different types of projects, from a city's building of a bridge to the investigation of faulty machinery in a factory.

There are three main formats to a progress report (Boyd, 2020), the first two of which have already been discussed.
1. Memo
2. Email/ letter
3. A formal report

How to write a progress report

As the first two formats have already been covered, this section will focus on how to construct a formal progress report. This is the most complex format of the three, and the one that you may need to bring out when dealing with an important client.

There are a number of important pointers to remember when you are creating a formal progress report.

- **Think about your audience!** Explain technical terms when needed.
- **Be unbiased.** State well evidenced claims rather than under-researched opinions.
- **Use diagrams.** Breaking up your text with charts or graphs can provide for a more engaging read.
- **Use concise language** (as always when writing technically).
- **Think about your report as a question and answer**. Imagine the questions that would be raised about the progress of this project (Balmaceda, 2018).

The next important step is structuring your piece. You will first need to consider whether this is a daily, weekly, or monthly report and who it is written for - will only one person be looking at this or a group of people (Balmaceda, 2018)?

Unlike a memo, which has a general and simple formulaic structure, you may wish to jazz up your progress report depending on your audience. This could include using colored text boxes or different fonts. There are plenty of templates available on office software that you can draw from.

1) The Progress, Plans, Problems structure

You can structure a progress report using the PPP (progress, plans, problems) method (Jõgi, 2020):

1. Introduction

This is where you will provide a brief summary of the contents of your progress report. Keep this to one or two paragraphs if possible.

2. Progress

Outline what you have achieved so far in this section. You may wish to organize this in a list form, such as tasks completed this month. This could look something like:

Tasks completed this month:

- Increased vegan food blog articles to 6.
- Finished the annual Christmas photoshoot.
- Collaborated with Beyoncé for online digital segment.
- Drew up plans for the revamping of second kitchen.

3. Plans

Here you will want to write about the goals to be achieved over the next window of time.

Goals for next month:

- Edit and format the Spring photoshoot.
- Edit and upload the Beyoncé digital segment.
- Get builders in to start revamping the second kitchen.
- Collaborate with Billie Eilish for digital segment.

---

4. Problems

Outline any obstacles to achieving your objectives here.

Potential obstacles and solutions:

- Billie Eilish's agent has not confirmed that she is available on the date that we have outlined.
- Solution: postpone this segment and request Adele to come in early.

---

2) Chronological progress report structure

Another possible way to organize a progress report is simply chronological (Mohan; Sharma, 2016, p.215). The idea behind a chronological structure is to base the report on how close to completion the project is. Generally speaking, progress reports should contain the following information:

- The title or name of the project
- Current date
- Details of the completed work
- Details of the work yet to be completed
- Target date of completion
- Additional information (if relevant)

Useful language

Remember to use simplified language in your short report.

In consequence of	Due to
Generate a list	Listed
Reach out to	Email
Things we hope to achieve	Goals
Ways that we can resolve things	Solutions

Exercises

1. Without checking, what are the PPP and how are they used?
2. Which of the following sentences would you expect to see on a meeting minutes report?
   - Present: Debra O, Sarah H, Linda M, Danny T, Tim P, Tim L, Tim H.
   - Sarah said that she had to leave early because she needed to attend to a family emergency.
   - All participants approved the motion that next week's meeting should be moved to the following week.
   - All participants approved the motion that the office should host a puppy and kittens workday.
   - Sarah said that she really likes puppies and kittens, so she gave a thumbs up to that idea.
   - All participants rejected the motion that employees work on Saturdays this month.
   - Minutes Approved By: Linda M.
3. How would you phrase a generic request that an action is taken at the end of a memo report?
4. What details are typically included in an expense report?

NOTES

Chapter 6:
Assembling Long Reports

This chapter deals with long reports, which will initially outline how to approach their general structure and then focus on more specific examples: feasibility and annual reports.

Both annual and feasibility reports have a major common characteristic, aside from being longer pieces than memos or minutes. These reports are interpretive in nature: they analyze a situation and formulate recommendations or goals.

General characteristics of long reports

Starting out: defining a purpose and an audience
The following section outlines the basic steps of long report writing. Whatever type of report that you are writing, the process should begin with the same general questions.

1. What is this report about?
2. Why is it needed?
3. Who is it for?

This step helps you establish what you are trying to write about. for whom, and what is at stake. Good writing should always hold something at stake, or in other words, have something to say -- make sure that you are writing for a defined purpose!

a) *What is the report about and why is it needed?*

If you have been provided with terms of reference, you should certainly spend some time on these before rushing to collect your data. Terms of reference (ToR) are usually a document which outlines the purpose, scope, and structure of a project. These could look something like the following:

> *University Education Committee (University of Bristol) appointed by the organization Senate, Terms of Reference (1 and 2)*

1. To develop and articulate the University's vision for education enhancement and innovation via the University's Education Strategy and maintain oversight of its delivery.
2. To make decisions on educational priorities, with the aim of enhancing the academic experience for students and with regard to the Education Strategy and the University's education-related risks and Strategic Performance Indicators (SPIs).

Do not hesitate to spend time analyzing the terms of reference. They should guide how you define the purpose of your report, which is obviously a very important preliminary step. Getting the focus of the report wrong would certainly set you back, so consider each instruction carefully.

b) *Who is it for?*
The terms of reference should inform you on who the report is addressed to. But on top of the information provided, you should always think about which category your audience fits in.
- Is your audience *external* or *internal*?
- Is your audience *vertically* or *laterally* situated relatively to you in the company's *hierarchy*?

- Does your audience include *shareholders*?
- Does your audience include *government officials*?
- Does your audience include *members of the public*?

Determining who your audience is, their background, and what information they may already have will help you find the right tone, style, and degree of formality.

How to make your report analytical

If your report requires you to handle data, whether qualitative or quantitative, it may be referred to as an *analytical* report. Shorter reports are rarely analytical, as they prioritize conciseness over detail. However, many types of reports can be analytical, as this is a general term: a report is analytical when its purpose is more than simply informative.

The findings and discussion section in a report is the heart of the analysis. This should detail the results you have found, which should then be discussed. This means that you should not only *describe* findings, but also analyze and interpret them. The hardest aspect of analytical writing is to avoid simply stating facts, and rather, to adopt a critical attitude towards your topic.

In order to shift your writing from descriptive or factual to analytical or critical, remember to:

- **Evaluate** significance. Instead of blandly stating "what happened", explain why it is important or relevant that it did.
- **Judge** the strengths and weaknesses of the information you have gathered. Be critical of your data: don't simply give a picture of the information you have, gauge its relevance, and critique its shortcomings. What does your data fail to encompass? Are there any inconsistencies?
- **Argue** in favor of a stance by weighing evidence. Compare and contrast data to try and discern the most satisfying solution.

Example: You work for the human resources department of a company. You are asked to write a report about the company's past hiring policy, with the goal of uncovering the most effective hiring strategy.

Descriptive writing:
This study measures the effectiveness of various hiring policies at company X in the past 10 years. Results show that LinkedIn is no longer the preferred or most effective platform from which to hire new employees. The different hiring strategies examined in this study consist of LinkedIn, Indeed, Smart Recruiters, Facebook as well as traditional recruitment agencies.

Improved analytical writing:
This study calculates the effectiveness of several hiring policies based on the renewal of recent recruits' probation period (or lack thereof) over the past 10 years at Company X. This timeline was chosen because of the popularization of other hiring platforms (Facebook, Indeed, Smart Recruiters) in the last decade, and its influence on hiring policies. Results indicate a drop in the effectiveness of the previously dominant platform LinkedIn.

Collecting data

After defining the purpose and audience of your report, the next step you need to think about is gathering the necessary information, which will form the basis of your analysis. The questions you should ask yourself are:

- What information do I need?
- Where can I get it?

Method of collecting data will very much depend on its nature. Different types of methods may include:

- Interviews
- Surveys and questionnaires
- Statistics
- Observation

More theoretical sources such as academic literature may be used, as well as archives and records. Whichever way of collecting information you choose, make sure to take notes and document your sources precisely. This will be important when writing up your report.

Sorting through material

After gathering your information, sorting through the most relevant sources and facts is the next step. It's not always easy when information on a particular theme is abundant, but you won't be able to integrate every source you have read or fact you have gathered in your report.

Try to bring together related facts or points. Make a list of information which seems to "go together"; these categories can help you come up with sections or chapters later in your report. If something doesn't fit into a category, it may have to be left out.

To ensure that your selected information is relevant, try and relate each point to the theme of your report. You can do this by formulating a sentence tying each fact or source of information to the overarching topic.

Planning your findings

So, it might seem strange to advise "planning" your findings, but you certainly need to have an idea of where you are headed before you start writing. Essentially, this is the way towards analyzing your data. Ask yourself:

1. What story does the data seem to tell?
2. How representative/reliable is your data?
3. What are its potential limitations?
4. Are there tensions/contradictions between some of the evidence?

Once you have simply described the data (1), you need to keep digging deeper. Acknowledging limitations (2 and 3) will always strengthen your report, and help you anticipate objections. On top of that, tensions in the data (4) are often the most interesting aspects: they allow you to develop a nuanced interpretation of the information you have collected.

Remember, all of these steps must always be connected to the aim and theme of the report. The findings section should be an answer to the question asked in your introduction.

Writing up!

By now, you should have a basic draft of your information and your analysis. It's time to start writing out the report properly. Remember the basic structure of the overall report and that of each section should be:

(1) Broadly introduce the matter
(2) Define the issues and key terms

(3) State your take/observation/interpretation
(4) Present supporting evidence
(5) Contrast with over evidence
(6) Conclude

By using this structure in each paragraph or section, you will be sure to write effectively, without losing sight of your topic. Concerning your writing style, use simple language and concise sentences, as is required by technical writing in general.

Reviewing and redrafting

Your first draft might need some sprucing up-- rewriting some sections is probably necessary to make sure the report forms a cohesive ensemble. While rereading the report, the questions you should ask yourself are "does this flow?" and "does this make sense?". Adding logical linking words can often help to ease transitions and clarify the argumentative structure.

Reason	Consequence	Contrast	Similarity/ addition	Concession	Comparison	Time
Because	Consequently	Nevertheless	In addition	Though	Rather	By the
Seeing that	As a result	However	Similarly	Even though	than	time
Since	In light of	Despite	Moreover	Although	Than	As
Why	So	In spite of	Likewise	While	Whereas	long
In order		Nonetheless	Equally			as
(that)		Unlike	Like			Before
			As well as			Once
						Still

Presentation and formatting

Once you are satisfied with the substance of your report, presentation should be your next concern. Consistency between headings should be checked, as well as page numbers. Also, remember to make sure your report complies with the formatting guidelines. Proofread the report, keeping an eye out for grammar, spelling, or punctuation mistakes.

Last but certainly not least, check and double-check your referencing! Citations should be accurate and include page numbers when direct quotes have been used. Refer to Chapter 1 for more detailed instructions on referencing.

These general steps apply to a variety of different long reports, but applications, purpose and process vary widely between different kinds of reports. So now, let's look at some more specific types of long reports.

Feasibility reports

What is a feasibility report?
This is where things get a bit more specific. A feasibility report or a feasibility study report (FSR) is a statement that tries to create a type of action. These are generated to help decision makers weigh up and choose between options by evaluating how desirable and practical a project is (Lumen, 2020). The usefulness of a feasibility report can span from planning a wedding to policies aimed at rehousing vulnerable persons.
A city council, for example, may want to know how the costs compare for different rehousing strategies. Furthermore, they may also want to know how the general public will react to different options. Providing a report analyzing these factors will go a long way in helping them to choose which action to pursue. It is also useful to understand how to compose a feasibility report as many of its parts are relevant in other areas. For

example, analyzing the feasibility of something is key to creating project proposals.

How to write a feasibility report

As a feasibility report is essentially an analysis of how good an option is, it is important that the writer includes the following considerations.

- **Consider alternatives**

A feasibility should be an unbiased analysis of an option. It is important, therefore, that alternatives are fully evaluated and considered rather than bulldozing one item through.

- **Think about your audience!**

Is your argument appropriate (Lumen, 2020)? How relevant is your analysis to the decision makers? In other words, think about the feasibility of your feasibility report. There would be no point, for example, in considering the feasibility of demolishing nationally protected homes and replacing them with apartment complexes in a democratic society.

- **Research your sources**

Decision makers will likely want assurance that the sources that you draw from to support your argument are credible (Lumen, 2020). One dodgy source can ruin the validity of your entire argument.

A feasibility report may be structured as follows. Remember, you may need to adjust depending on what is most relevant to your piece and that the actual layout of a feasibility report will vary from project to project.

Front matter

A title page:

A contents page:

| FEASABILITY STUDY

Project Name

Presented To:
Company Name
Address
Date

Presented By:
Author's Name
Job Position
Email | FEASABILITY STUDY

TABLE OF CONTENTS

 |

Report Body

1. Introduction

Introduce the problem and the proposed solution (Boyd, 2020).

Example: this might cover the housing shortage for vulnerable persons in a city and the proposal to build new homes on brown belt land.

2. Background

This section will provide important contextual information (Boyd, 2020).

Example: this may outline the city councils housing policy, the government's housing policy, the history of the problem of housing vulnerable persons, and any other relevant information.

3. Criteria

Next, you may want to outline the criteria for your ideal outcomes in a separate section (Lumen, 2020). The criteria are descriptions of how you are evaluating the feasibility of a potential solution (Boyd, 2020).

Example: you may be evaluating a potential housing policy based on economic, political, and environmental criteria.

4. Method

Including a methods section will up your credibility as an author; state the sources that you drew from here and why (Lumen, 2020).

Example: you may have drawn from governmental datasets which are a well-respected resource.

5. Overview of Alternative Options

Summarize the main points of alternative options (Lumen, 2020).

Organize this in a clear and understandable format.

Example: this may include building homes on brown belt land or creating a scheme for individuals to offer a bedroom to vulnerable persons.

6. Evaluation

This will be the main chunk of your report. Here, you will evaluate the options that are being considered with the criteria that you have specified (Lumen, 2020). It is also useful to compare the recommended option to the current situation (Boyd, 2020).

Example: you may wish to compare building homes on brown belt sites with the costs of renting temporary accommodation. Remember to support this option with thorough evidence.

7. Conclusions

Outline the conclusion that you have drawn. How were the alternatives evaluated (Lumen, 2020)? Which option comes out on top?

8. Recommendations

Finish up with your recommendation. Drawing from your own experience, knowledge, and evaluation of the options, which should be adopted by the decision makers?

Example: having observed the adoption of this policy in other cities and given that it is the most economically and politically feasible, you have concluded that homes should be built on brown belt land.

Back Matter

Reference Page:

Appendix: Provide more detailed discussions on the

criteria used in feasibility analysis, as well as examples of the criteria (Lewinson, 2012).

For more information on how to reference, see Chapter 1.	FEASIBILITY STUDY APPENDIX Appendix A: Survey Questions Appendix B: Links to News Articles Appendix C: Differences Between The Environmental Impacts of Brown Belt Building and Green Belt Building Database Appendix D: An Example of Brown Belt Building

Useful language
There are a number of technical terms that are frequently used in feasibility reports.

Economic feasibility Political feasibility Environmental feasibility Recommendations Evaluations Methodology Approach	Identified solution Cost- effectiveness Practicality

Annual reports

What is an annual report?

Annual reports are essentially a summary of an organization's mission and history, which outline their achievements over the past year (McGurgan, 2020). They are basically a report on the "health" of an organization, written for the benefit of the media, analysts, the community, stakeholders, and shareholders (McGurgan, 2020).

Knowing how to write an annual report can also be useful when constructing other similar pieces. The evaluative nature of an annual report can, for example, help when writing up summaries. Furthermore, public companies in the US are legally required to produce comprehensive annual reports, under the Securities and Exchange Commission (FreshBooks, 2020). Though smaller companies and non-profit organizations are not legally required to, it has become standard practice amongst most sectors.
They come in an array of formats, which can range from simple documents to highly produced booklets. The main purposes of an annual report are to:

- **Summarize financial information**
This is an outline of an organization's financial year, which helps the audience to know how much the organization owns and how much it owes, its capacity to make money and how it funds its operations (McGurgan, 2020).

- **Showcase achievements**
Aside from financial achievements, other achievements are showcased in an annual report. This may include advances made in research or awards the organization has received (McGurgan, 2020). This section will help any investors or participants in your organization feel reassured about their involvement.

- **Promote the organization**

Annual reports are also used to promote an organization. Emphasis on a specific achievement, such as distributing x resources to vulnerable people, is placed to market the organization. Within this, you may want to include the testimonies of clients, employees or other individuals and groups who have been impacted by your mission. This section will add a necessary human touch to the financial talk.

- **Provide additional information**

You may wish to include key figures in your organization, such as the board of directors, a brief bit of information and their photographs. Additionally, a letter to an organization's shareholders should be included at the start of an annual report (McGurgan, 2020). This letter should be written by the highest position in your organization, such as the Chief Exec, and will outline key points, including an overview of profits, and information about any upcoming plans.

How to write an annual report

When writing an annual report, it is important to keep a few things in mind.

- **Outline and emphasize your key message**

Your annual report is not merely a bland outline of your organization's financial progress. It is also an opportunity to sell yourself. Make sure to tie your main accomplishments to descriptions of your activities, goals, and plans.

- **Be organized**

You cannot include everything in your annual report - doing so would be overwhelming and off-putting to your reader. Before your write up, make sure to plan what you are including. Apart from the basics, your annual report should have a key thread - a storyline tying it together (FreshBooks, 2020).

- **Be honest**

Transparency is key to gaining the trust of your reader. If you skew your report to include only the positives, you could find yourself in a troublesome situation when word gets out about some of your issues. Remember to approach your report in a professional and unbiased manner. Don't oversell your accomplishments and don't omit any issues that you've faced (FreshBooks, 2020).

- **Use an engaging design**

Your report should not be one giant block of text. Aside from including too much information, the next no-no is to put off your reader before they've even started reading. Report styles will vary from organization to organization, but it good to break up and elaborate on your message by using headings and subheadings, infographics, and colored text boxes and quotes. The following outlines the general structure of an annual report. Some components will be more applicable to for-profit businesses -- the next section will outline how to make necessary adjustments for non-profits.

1. The Chairperson's Letter

This is the first thing that your reader will see and will set the tone of your entire piece. A brief overview of key developments, financials and objectives should be provided. Outline the main challenges and successes of an organization.

2. Table of Contents

See "Feasibility Reports" for an example.

3. Profile

This section provides the bigger picture of your organization, including your vision and central objectives. The face of the organization should also be included, such as details of directors, the registered office, investor profiles, products/ services which are a major revenue source, profile of competitors and any risk factors (FreshBooks, 2020).

4. Management Discussion and Analysis

This will move onto the business side, providing an overview of performance over the past three years which may include a discussion of sales, income, and profits.

Additional information which may be important should be included here. This may include any new products or services that have been developed, business acquisitions or shifts in marketing strategies (FreshBooks, 2020).

5. Achievements

You may wish to include an additional section outlining your organization's achievements over the past year. Include stories, photographs, or small case studies if appropriate.

6. Financial Statements

The finances are usually the most important part of an annual report, which provide an analysis of financial performance to your reader.

Financial statements will usually include a

- Balance sheet
- Financial statement
- Cash flow statement
- Income statement
- Financial notes outlining the organizations accounting methods
- Additional information such as pension plan contributions (McGurgan, 2020), or comments by auditors.

The dilemma for non-profits

Though it is not legally required for non-profits to produce annual reports in the US, it is highly recommended. These documents are often important to building trust with your donors and supporters.

The main dilemma that non-profits face when writing annual reports, however, is what should be included? When so many guides are geared towards responding to investors and shareholders, it can be difficult to determine what should and should not be prioritized in your report.

Here are some key tips for non-profits:

- **Do explain your financials**

You may not be working for profit, but that doesn't mean that you shouldn't include the details of your finances. Differently to an annual report that is geared towards investors, however, it is likely that your donors will have less of a grasp on the financial mumbo jumbo. You should include a paragraph or two in plain language which simply explains the content of your graphs, tables, or charts (Miller, 2020). It may also be useful to include some infographics to engage your audience -- more on this later

- **Include donor lists**

Swap out the investor profiles for those of your donors. Recognizing those who give to your organization is one of the most important purposes of an annual report for non-profits. However, it is important to strike a balance between listing donors and the rest of your report's content. If your list is too long, consider reorganizing your layout or scaling back a bit (Miller, 2020).

- **Emphasize and personalize your achievements**

Your achievements section should occupy more space than in a company's annual report. Include more personal stories and examples which will relate to your donors. Additionally, this section should outweigh your financial achievements. Donors want to know what is being done with your money, not how you raised it (Miller, 2020).

- **Include photos**

Many of your readers will simply flick through your report -- it is most effective to catch their attention with the use of photos. These can help to accessibly demonstrate the story that your organization is telling. Remember to include captions which connect your photographs to an achievement or goal (Miller, 2020).

Useful language

Here is a more detailed breakdown of the standard sections in a long technical report, and the language that is conventionally used.

- **Title page**: The title of your report should be as short and to the point as it can be.

- **Terms of reference**: if writing a report in response to a request, you may be provided with terms of reference. These should specify what you should write the report about and how you should write it. The terms of reference are there to help you define the scope and the purpose of your report.

- **Summary**: a synthesis of the contents of the report.

- **Table of contents**: at the beginning of the report, a list of the sections covered.

- **Introduction:** preliminary section broadly presenting the topic at hand.

- **Methods/Procedure:** section detailing the process of data collection.

- **Findings**: section focusing on the description of the data.
- **Discussion/Recommendations**: conclusions drawn from the data.

- **Conclusion**: overall remarks on the topic and the observations it invites.

- **Bibliography/References**: list of consulted sources.

- **Appendices:** additional detailed documents too long to be included in the body of the report, such as drawings, tables o data or graphs.

- **Acknowledgements**: section to acknowledge the help of others in writing your report.

- **Glossary of technical terms:** list defining technical terms in the report.

Exercises
1. What are the four main purposes of an annual report?
2. You are a non-profit organization which works to end homelessness. What could be some of the key achievements that you would emphasize in your annual report? How would you present these?
3. You are writing a feasibility report on the potential for local governments to reclaim abandoned homes to rehouse homeless individuals. What feasible aspects would you need to consider?
4. Thinking about this same example, write up the first few lines on your "recommendations" section for this policy.
5. What is the purpose of a justification report?
6. What are the main differences between descriptive and analytical writing?

NOTES

_____

_____

_____

_____

Chapter 7:
Assembling Proposals

What is a proposal?

Next up is proposals. A proposal (sometimes referred to as a justification report) is a bid to complete something for someone. It essentially asks an audience to fund or approve a project (McMurrey, 2020). These will often consist of a variety of other components such as recommendations, technical background, feasibility, and survey results (McMurrey, 2020), however a proposal is different from these individual parts. Whilst a feasibility report outlines how feasible a course of action is, for example, a proposal asks for a decision on whether this action can be undertaken.

When writing a proposal, think about what you will need to include so that your reader can make an informed decision. It is important that you consider your PATs here -- what information will be most effectively relayed to your specific audience?

Pertinent to this consideration is the type of proposal that you are creating. The situations that you may be submitting a proposal in can vary widely. A company may send out a request for proposals (RFP), for example, or you may be pitching a proposal to your manager at work (McMurrey, 2020). The following explain more about the different proposals that you may encounter and how to approach them.

- **Solicited proposals**

This is a proposal where the recipient has made a request, such as an RFP. These will often be advertised on company websites or across other print/ digital mediums. Organizations or individuals who are interested in the project will then write proposals, and the company making the request will draw up a contract for the selected candidate (McMurrey, 2020). Solicited proposals aren't always as grandiose, however. You may be asked by your manager to submit a proposal for a project at your workplace. Key to the solicited proposal is that it is one made through a request.

- **Unsolicited proposals**

Intuitively, an unsolicited proposal is the opposite of a solicited one; the intended recipient has not made a request for a proposal and this has been independently initiated. In an unsolicited proposal, more attention is often paid to outlining why a problem exists that must be resolved in the first place.

- **Internal proposals**

An internal proposal is one made within your organization. These will often include less personal information, such as your work experience or qualifications, as your employer will already know this.

- **External proposals**

As it sounds, to propose something externally is to submit something from one entity to another (McMurrey, 2020). For example, a freelance consultant may contact a company which has put out an RFP.

How to write a proposal?
Some of the most salient characteristics of proposals include (Eggins, M., 2020):

- **Concise, straightforward writing.**
This is a general characteristic of all technical writing. But proposals, in particular, are written for an audience who may only have time to hastily skim through your report. It's all the more important to deliver your message as concisely as you can!

- **Well-defined scope.**
As well as targeted to a specific audience, your proposal should have a precisely targeted subject. Proposals are not written to ponder a thorny theoretical issue; their sole purpose is to offer clear solutions to outlined problems.

- **Format properly.**
The concise and on-message nature of proposals is enabled by strict formatting. Clear headlines should be used to delineate different sections. Short paragraphs can be used in moderation, to facilitate the reading process.

- **Use images.**
Graphics can be included to illustrate the proposals main points and make the piece more readable.

The sections of your proposal will vary depending on the area that you specialize in and the type of proposal that you are submitting. However, the following is a fairly standard layout that can be easily adjusted accordingly.

---

1. Introduction

Your introduction should immediately indicate that you are writing a proposal for a particular project (Morgan, 2020). It should then briefly summarize the contents of your proposal and persuade your audience to continue reading and consider your project.

Example: if you are proposing a screenplay for a movie production grant, you may state that your screenplay fills a gap in the market by focusing on class relations in contemporary Japanese society.

2. Background

After you have written your introduction, you will need to set the scene for your proposal. The background section is there to demonstrate why your project is needed - what current issues exist that need to be resolved? You may wish to draw from relevant literature or surrounding information.

Remember, this section is typically longer for unsolicited proposals but is necessary regardless of the proposal type. A background is also a chance for you to demonstrate your perspective on a particular issue and how you might approach it.

Example: movies centered on contemporary Japanese society often eliminate class as a focal point in topical considerations.

3. Feasibility and benefits of proposed work

Here you will go through the pros and cons of your proposed work. You may wish to refer back to the section on "Feasibility reports" for more advice on this topic. It is important to remember that a proposal is a highly persuasive piece. Though you should include potential

---

disadvantages, emphasis should be placed on why your idea should be adopted. Argue in favor of your project, such as a discussion on the likelihood of its success (McMurrey, 2020). Again, this is more important in an unsolicited proposal.

Example: it may be difficult to reach a large audience due to the specificity of your movie subject, however class relations are near universally felt and there is widespread international interest in Japanese culture.

4. Proposed work

This section should outline the probable outcomes of your proposed work and go into more details about your suggested measures.

Example: different steps in the movie production will be achieved at different dates. Selecting the production crew will be followed by organizing the production set, completing a first draft, a re-draft, a final draft, and the release of the film.

5. Method

How will you go about completing your proposed project? What is the approach that you will adopt? This section, like the rest of your piece, can be highly persuasive in demonstrating how you think and establishing your knowledge around a subject.

Example: you will employ a special consultatory group of Japanese individuals from differing class groups to comment on the production of your movie.

6. Schedule

This is not merely detailing when your project will be finished. A schedule outlines when key accomplishments will be achieved.

Example: your final movie draft will be finished in fall 2020 and will be ready for release in the following spring.

7. Costs and resources

Here you will detail the costs of your proposed project. External proposals may list estimated hours and rate per hour, as well as the standard estimate for equipment and supply costs and a total sum (McMurrey, 2020).

8. Conclusion

Here you will summarize the contents of your proposal and reiterate its positives. You can also encourage your reader to contact you to go through the project in more detail, state why you are the best candidate or the job and emphasize the benefits of the project.

Exercises

1. You are putting forward an unsolicited proposal on why your organic range of cat food should be stocked by a leading supermarket. Write the first few lines of your introduction.
2. Using the same project example, write the key points of your background section.
3. List all the potential readers of a proposal for the following RFPs.
   - A school has put out an RFP for a new curriculum for its drama department.
   - A think tank has put out an RFP for a demographic survey project.
   - A leading aquatics retail chain has put out an RFP for a improved storage system for tropical fish.

4. You are submitting an external proposal on the installation of solar powered tropical fish tanks for a leading aquatics retail chain. List the potential costs and resources needed for this project.

NOTES

_____

_____

_____

_____

_____

_____

_____

_____

_____

_____

_____

Chapter 8:
Assembling Summaries

What is a summary?

The purpose of a summary is pretty explicit - it is used to inform a reader about something they have not read, seen, or heard. In fact, the word "abstract" comes from the Latin word "abstractum", which is defined as a condensed version of a longer piece of writing (Mukhlis, 2015). In general terms, then, this could include a summary of a 600-page romantic space thriller or a presentation on how to build your own tiny house. In technical writing terms, however, summaries tend to fall into one of three categories: descriptive abstracts, informative abstracts, and executive summaries (Sweat, 2020).

These are essentially short overviews of documents (usually reports) to enable a reader to decide whether to read on. For example, companies sorting through RFP proposals will find a summary useful so they can immediately decide if a proposal is relevant or applicable to their organisation.

Descriptive Abstracts

What is a descriptive abstract?

The main role of descriptive abstracts is to provide a general overview of a documents central purpose and its content. Key is their descriptive nature; they are used to describe and introduce a text, and do not provide extensive information, conclusions, or recommendations. They are topic focussed rather than detail oriented.

Because of this, descriptive abstracts are usually very short - around 100 words or less. They tend to be placed on the title page of a text or at the top of the first page.

How to write a descriptive abstract

The content and style of your descriptive abstract is highly dependent on the type of work that you are summarizing. You may be writing a report summarising an experiment for a scientific journal or an annual report for a new app start up. It's important, therefore, to adapt your piece accordingly. In genera there are a number of things to bear in mind when writing your descriptive abstract:

- **Describe your project!** Make sure to describe what you are doing rather than what you are doing the project on! No need for an elaborate background description.

- **Be succinct.** You are providing a brief description of your work without going into too much detail. Your reader will still need to read your main work to get the bigger picture (Hartwell, 2020)!

- **Draw from your headings!** Descriptive abstracts are introductory and general. Headings usually supply this information and can be utilised in your abstract (Hartwell, 2020).

- **Start with a bang.** Your abstract should draw the reader in - your first sentence is key to this (Hartwell, 2020)!

The following sections could be included in your abstract (Mukhlis, 2015). Remember, these do not have to be included in any particular order.

1. Purpose

Why did you produce your piece? What were the key objectives?
Example (proposal): According to the 2016 Annual Beverage Survey, individuals across a wide range of demographics are seeking alternative beverages to their traditional counterparts. This has opened a gap in the market for new and innovative products.

2. Focus of piece

What is the main message of your piece?
Example: Libby's Coftea Oxford hopes to break into this market space with a range of high quality, local and ethically sourced products.

3. Overview of contents (if necessary)

What is included in your piece?
Example: This report demonstrates the competitive advantages to investing in Libby's Coftea. As the sole company in the coffee-tea industry, Libby's Coftea is uniquely positioned for expansion. Furthermore, our current growth projections forecast our first 6-months sales values at $2,000,000.

Informative abstracts

What is an informative abstract?

When it comes to longer documents, however, descriptive abstracts rarely suffice to provide enough information to encourage the reader to go on. Texts longer than ten pages, therefore, typically include an informative abstract. These are the most common types of abstract used in reports.

An informative abstract provides a summary of the most important points in a text. They are informative, meaning they provide information about the content rather than a mere description. This may include:

- Major points
- Results
- Conclusions
- Recommendations

These types of abstracts are also a lot longer than descriptive abstracts, occupying up to 10% of a document's total word count.

How to write an informative abstract

Informative extracts must be both succinct and explanatory. It is essential, then, that they are well thought through pieces. Here are some important tips (Indiana University, 2011):

- **Relevance.** Only include information from the document that is summarized!
- **Be concise.** Include the most important information and keep it brief.
- **Clarity.** Don't waffle and don't include elaborate terms. Keep your language plain!

An informative abstract may include the following parts (Indiana University, 2011). Remember, the headings provided here are for guidance purposes only - you will not need to include them in your final piece!

1. Purpose

This is the central reason for your work. If you conducted an experiment or research, you may wish to include your hypothesis here.

Example (feasibility report): This report analyses the feasibility of building homes on brown belt sites to address the increasing housing shortage for vulnerable people in Birmingham. This work was commissioned by Representative M. Bliss for the Birmingham City Council. Our initial hypothesis was that building homes on brown belt sites across the city and its outer perimeters would be the most feasible solution to this problem.

2. Methodology

These are the techniques deployed to produce your results/ conclusions.

Example: We conducted quantitative and qualitative analyses to ascertain the economic, political and social feasibility of four different potential solutions: i) building new homes on brown belt sites, ii) reclaiming homes that have been abandoned for more than five years, iii) renting homes from private landlords through the city council, iv) renting hotel and hostel rooms through the city council. These analyses involved public surveys across the city, literature reviews and housing and council funding data set analyses.

3. Results

Discuss the results of your report. What did you find?

Example: In terms of economic feasibility, we found reclaiming abandoned homes to be the most effective solution and renting hotel and hostel rooms to be the least. In terms of both political and social feasibility, building new homes was the most and renting hotel and hostel rooms the least. Renting homes from private landlords through the city council was the second least feasible option on all accounts.

4. Conclusions

Discuss the evaluation of your findings here, as well as the implications of these findings. You may wish to address your initial hypothesis here.

Example: Overall, this study found building new homes on brown belt sites to be the most feasible solution to the housing shortage, supporting our initial hypothesis. This is followed by, in order of overall feasibility: reclaiming abandoned homes, renting from private landlords and renting hotel and hostel rooms. We would encourage the Birmingham City Council to draw from these conclusions in their own future policy recommendations and implement building strategies accordingly.

Executive summaries

What is an executive summary?

An executive summary goes even further than an informative abstract; it is a short document or a longer section of a document which provides an overview of the main reports of a report. An important differentiator is how much information is included: an executive summary should enable a reader to understand what a report discusses, without having to read it. Executive summaries are, therefore, often produced for businesses, such as when putting forward a recommendation or proposal. The role of an executive summary is to summarize the main points in a document. It should (Ashford University, 2020):

- Reiterate the purpose
- Highlight the main points
- Describe any results/ conclusions/ recommendations

How to write an executive summary

There are a number of things to remember when writing an executive summary (Forsey, 2020):

1. **Remember your PAT!** (*Purpose, Audience, Tone*, see in Chapter 2)

Focussing on the purpose of your writing will help produce a cohesive piece and allow you to produce the story that you want to tell. What does your organization do? Why do you do it? Also think about who it is you are writing to and how you are writing - what information is most likely to resonate with them? Is your company more informal or formal?

2. **Be thorough.**

Though an executive summary is considerably shorter than the rest of your piece, this doesn't render it any less important. In fact, because this may be the deciding factor as to whether someone reads your document or not, it is even more essential that this is well-researched and thought through. A proposal summary to a leading company should include financial considerations, competitor analysis and your key findings. Think about it like a company pitch.

3. **Don't be corny.**

As a general rule of thumb for any technical writing, avoid clichés at all costs! These are very off-putting to a reader, who will struggle to take you seriously.

4. **Leave it until the end.**

Though an executive summary usually comes at the beginning of a piece, it should be the item that you write last. This is fairly obvious: you won't be able to summarize something if there is nothing to summarize. Nevertheless, it is important to keep this in mind as it may be tempting to whack this out at the beginning.

Now that you know how to approach your writing, it is time to think about how you are going to put this together. The following template is for a conventional business plan and, like any template, should be adjusted to your particular project (Forsey, 2020). If you are an established organization or starting up, for example, you will clearly need to make some changes. If you are the latter, you will likely not have as much information as an established organization (Lumen, 2020). In this instance, it is important to place more emphasis on your experience and background - what has led you to this project? Include detailed market analysis, such as how you will fill a gap in the market and how you will succeed in this (Lumen, 2020).

Executive Summary

Our Mission

This should include the name, location, and mission of your company.

Example: Libby's Coftea Oxford is dedicated to releasing new and innovative beverage products onto the market. Our unique coffee-tea blend is incorporated into a range of items, including Coftea Cakes and Coftea Sodas, and hopes to expand into Coftea Bread. We are committed to producing high quality products transparently and ethically: our ingredients are 100% Fairtrade and renewably sourced. As we are the only coffee-tea focussed company in the food and drink industry, we anticipate very mild to no competition and are assured that we can develop a strong market presence.

Our Company

This should include a description of your organization such as management and a brief history.

Example: Libby's Coftea was founded in Oxford, UK, in 2015 by Libby Chan. She first began selling her unique coffee-tea blend at local markets and then began to supply local independent cafes across the city. In 2016, after the extensive expansion of her business, she moved her coffee-tea blending facility from her home to a locally based warehouse which now employs over 30 full-time staff. Prior to developing Libby's Coftea Oxford, Libby Chan worked as a fine tea expert at Cowley Road Fine Tea's.

Alongside Libby Chan, Libby's Coftea Oxford has a board of advisors. These are:

1. Felicity Chan, Director of Digital Marketing at Kuma Kitchens Ltd.
2. Zoe Paris, Food Developer at Kuma Kitchens Ltd.

Our Product

This should cover what your product is and where it fits in the market.

Example: We offer coffee-tea products ranging from Coftea Cakes to Coftea Sodas. Our customers are ethically oriented, eco-conscious and have a taste for high quality alternative products. We will produce a range of Coftea Bread which will both appeal to our regular consumer base and reach more diverse customers through the expansion into supermarkets. We will prioritise high-quality, ethical, and eco-friendly production whilst ensuring decent prices.

Competitive Advantages

Here, talk about how your product differs from other competitors.

Example: Whilst there is an extensive market for alternative coffee and tea blends, there are no company's which combine the two together.

This gives Libby's Coftea a distinct competitive advantage, placing us as the only brand in the coffee-tea industry. Furthermore, market research [see Section 7] shows that consumers have an increasing appetite for alternatives to traditional blends.

Financial Considerations

What are your sales projections and other important costs?

Example: Our sales projections for the first 6 months are $2,000,000. We expect a 40% growth over the next 3 years. By year 2, we expect 20% gross margins. We have 30 full-time staff. Their salary will be $80,000.

Financing Requirements

How many funds will you require? How much has already been invested/ supplemented?

Example: We hope to raise $300,000 to start-up this project. We have already received an investment of $125,000 towards these costs.

Useful language

As mentioned, a summary is used to draw your reader in. Here are some useful terms:

• Project	• Conduct
• Growth	• Demonstrate
• Expansion	• Present
• Prioritise	• Found
• Ensure	• Conclude
• Encourage	
• Support	

Exercises

1. You are writing a summary for a 100-page business plan. Which summary type is most appropriate to your piece and why?
2. You need to write a brief summary for a one-page recommendation. Which summary type is most appropriate to your piece and why?
3. You're writing a descriptive abstract for a proposal to increase rubbish collection times, written to your local authority. Write your opening line for this abstract.
4. Without checking, what are the main sections you may include in an informative abstract?

NOTES

_____

_____

_____

_____

_____

_____

_____

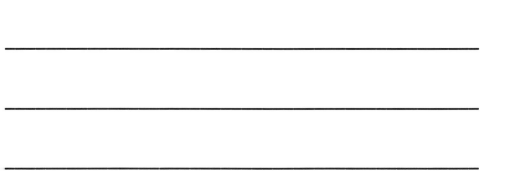

Chapter 9:
Assembling User Manuals

A user manual is a guide, detailing instructions the reader should follow in order to complete a task. This might range from building a flat-pack table to installing software on your laptop: user manuals are a widely ranging type of document. Above all, their main characteristic is *clarity*. The purpose of a user manual is to instruct on how to achieve a task, so breaking down steps rigorously and leaving no room for confusion is of the utmost importance.

As usual, remember your Purpose, Audience, and Tone (see Chapter 2). While the purpose of a manual is informative, your audience consists of the product users, and your tone should always be short and neutral.

How to structure a user manual

The following section describes the sections typically included in a user manual.

Title

As always with technical writing, the title of a use manual should be clear and informative. It should most prominently emphasize the *product* and service provided.

- **Table of contents**

The table of contents is included in a manual to help the user find information easily. If you are writing an online user manual, the table of contents should always be interactive, so that the reader can access the relevant section in a simple click.

- **"About this product"**

The "about this product" section should inform on the name and version of the product. It may also define technical vocabulary or provide any information necessary to use the manual.

- **Overview / Product features**

Usually, the product overview thanks the client for choosing the product, and presents its main features, or in other words, what it does.

- **What's in the box?**

What's in the box? is a list of the materials contained in the product's box. In the case of a manufacturing error resulting in a missing piece, the user can inform the company with this information.

- **Glossary**

If your manual uses technical vocabulary, it is customary to include a glossary. It is usually included at the end of the document, if it is present at all.

- **Specifications**

The specifications are the technical features of the product, such as its weight, operating temperature, or sound emission levels.

This section is not of much interest to users, but simply provides a technical description of the product.

How to deliver instructions
Here are some important tips on delivering instructions:

- **Break down the steps.**
Steps should be divided into sub-steps, or the smallest unit of action required at a time. Sentences should only describe one instruction at a time.

- **Organize steps in chronological order.**
The structure of each sentence should parallel the order of the action. Do not write "Cut the purple wire once you have pushed the red button". This would naturally confuse the reader as to the order of the process. Rather, write: "(1) Push the red button and (2) then cut the purple wire".

- **Do not overwhelm your reader with unnecessary information.**
Information should be provided at the exact point in the process where it is necessary. Remember, your reader may be skimming through the manual and forget information which was mentioned earlier on.

- **Get rid of your assumptions.**
If you are writing a user manual, you are probably very familiar with the product which you are advising on. However, it's unlikely that all of your readers will know much about it. So, things which are obvious to you are not necessarily obvious to your reader. To avoid packing hidden assumptions into your manual, try to write as if you knew nothing on the subject of the user guide.

- **Refer to materials clearly.**

If tasks involve using materials provided with the product (such as screws, cables, etc.), these should be numbered or lettered. This avoids confusion for the reader when detailing instructions on what materials to use.

- **Active, concise language.**

Use verbs rather than nouns and avoid long sentences. Always use an imperative verb like "attach", "combine", "download", rather than a phrase such as "you should", "you have to", or you must" to deliver an instruction. This avoids unnecessarily addressing the user.

Troubleshooting

The troubleshooting section in a user manual presents common problems that users may be met with. This part of your user manual should aim to predict problem scenarios or questions and provide clear answers or solutions.

Formulating potential problems or questions in the first person, as if voicing the problem from the user's perspective, is a good way to make your troubleshooting section sound friendly (Wallwork, 2014).

Example:

1. My TV will not turn on.
2. My TV screen is flickering.

The possible solutions can be formulated as questions or steps to fix the problem.

1. My TV will not turn on

> Is your TV plugged in? If you have a socket switch, is it turned on?
>
> If you can, plug your TV in another socket.
>
> If you are using the TV remote control, check the batteries. Use the main TV control button instead.

Organizing your troubleshooting section into categories will make it easier for users to find the solution to their problem. Avoid long lists with no distinction between different types of problems, as they tend to cause further confusion. Rather, a successful troubleshooting section should also aim to provide answers to problems in an organized manner.

Subsections in a TV user guide, for instance, could be split into:

- On screen messages
- TV settings
- WIFI & network
- Remote control
- General problems

Warnings and safety instructions

To express warnings or deliver safety instructions, it is most effective to use the imperative mood. Protecting the manufacturer from customer complaints, and of course, informing the user of any potential hazards, requires clarity. Using unambiguous terms and a single format is the best way to achieve this.

Avoid multiplying different formulations, such as "we strongly recommend that you do not" or "it is preferable not to". Instead, stick to "Do not" (Wallwork, 2014). To emphasize your point even more, you can also use "never" followed by an imperative verb.

It's also helpful to outline possible consequences of disregarding a warning. This can help make the reader more aware, and therefore more likely to follow safety instructions. Manuals use "may", "could", "might", or "will" to express various degrees of risk that danger could occur, if instructions are ignored.

Example:

- Do not place your TV set near a source of heat, such as next to a radiator, or in direct sunlight.
- Do not expose your TV set to water. If your set gets wet, immediately contact our helpline.
- Never insert any metallic objects into the openings of your TV set. This could cause an electric shock.

Exercises

1. Have a look at the instructions below. What are some of the main problems that you can identify and what would you change?

Instructions to secure a TV set onto a wall.

1.	You need to use the right screws to fasten the brackets to the wall. Make sure the wall you have selected does not require you to use wall plugs to complete this step. Also, you should have drilled holes into your wall in a good spot for your TV. See the section on "Where to place your TV".
2.	Then using the other screws, fit the other brackets onto the TV. To know which screws to use, you have to go to the section "attaching the TV on a wall" section of this guide.
3.	Now you should be ready to tie the brackets on the wall and the brackets on the TV together. To do that, you should use strong string provided in the box. Tie the string as tightly as you can.

4.	You should make sure that the TV is close enough to the wall, so that it can't fall back.
5.	Now that you have tied the strong, the brackets on the wall and the ones on the TV should be level. You need to make sure that the string isn't loose or floppy in the middle, otherwise your set won't be secure.

NOTES

Chapter 10:
How To Web Write

What is web writing?
A website content writer is somewhat newer to the field of technical writing but is fast becoming an increasingly sought after and lucrative profession. In short, web content writers specialise in producing writing for websites. This could be writing articles for a vegan lifestyle site, producing informative content for a hedge fund firm, or creating overviews on national population statistics. In summary, web content writers are all over the place.

Despite this, there are clearly defined forms of web content to consider, as well as distinctly different writing styles. Different forms of web content include (Gotter, 2017):
1. Blogs
2. Longform content
3. Case studies
4. White papers
5. eBooks
6. Infographics (see Chapter 9)
7. Template and checklist downloads

The varied character of web writing also means that it must be highly attuned to target audiences, especially for businesses looking to attract consumers. Web writers, therefore, have to adapt their style and content to cater to specific online audiences. One important way to do this is through the use of SEOs.

The SEO mystery

What is SEO?

Many people have heard the term SEO thrown around, but don't fully understand what it means. In fact, without elaboration, it can seem like nonsense computer-speak. But, not to fear! Search Engine Optimisation is a lot easier to grasp than it sounds.

In a nutshell, SEO is the practice of increasing the quantity and quality of traffic to a website through "organic search engine results" (Moz, 2020). Put simply, it is the practice of attracting more people, who are genuinely interested in your website, without using paid advertisements-- that's the organic part. Drawing an audience organically, therefore, means that you are getting unpaid traffic through search engine results pages (SERPs) (Moz, 2020). This is clearly desirable for any organization hoping to up visitors to their site.

But how does it work? Results pages on search engines such as Google don't just magically appear. They are organised by a variety of factors; SEO is the process of optimising this organisation to your website's advantage. Explaining the algorithms at play here could fill an entire book and are held secret by many big tech companies. In brief, search engines will scan (or "crawl") different websites to deliver the most relevant results -- largely determined by particular phrases and keywords (Sherman, 2019).

How to practice SEO

Now we know how it works, how do we actually practice SEO (Sherman, 2019)?

1. Improve your content

The most important factor to the success of your site is focussing on your content. This is the backbone of your website – no amount of graphic fluff can distract from a poorly written piece.

- **Create high quality content.**

The more quality content, the better. An abundance of relevant pieces will propel you up the search engine ranks, and good quality work will keep your audience engaged and sticking around for longer. Make sure to diversify your content and ensure that it is well-written and topical, in order to avoid it going stale.

- **Include key words and phrases.**

Another SEO technique is to use key words and phrases generously across your site. These are the words or phrases that you would expect a user to deploy in their initial search. Create content around these key words and phrases and make sure to use them throughout your work - but use them wisely! Including 10 or so keywords can suffocate and unfocus your piece. Instead, it is better to build your content around one or two keywords to ensure that your piece is focussed and relevant.

- **Keep it new.**

To optimise your results, you need to keep things rolling. Relying on old and outdated content is a sure way to keep your numbers low. However, you don't always need to keep purging out entirely new content. Updating posts with re-writes and new information or statistics will also increase your search engine ranking.

2. **Make technical adjustments**

Once you've got good quality content down, you need to think about how to organise it. SEO moves beyond the purely written stuff - it's also the presentation.

- **Tag your title.**

This is the HTML element which is the clickable headline for your page (Moz, 2020). Include keywords relating to the topic of your content as well as your organisation's name. For example, the title of a guide on how to grow tomatoes may be "Kuma Kitchens: Top 10 Tips to Growing Fresh and Juicy Tomatoes".

- **Include subheadings!**

Sub-headings break up your work into easily digestible chunks and encourage a visitor to read on. These can be tagged using H2 and H3 tags. Whilst H2 tags act as your main subheadings, H3 tags act as subheadings for your H2s. Like your title, remember to include keywords and relevant information.

- **Write a meta description.**

This is another HTML element which appears under your title tag in search engines. It is highly influential to whether a potential visitor clicks on your site (Moz, 2020), and is what appears when someone shares your page. This should include a brief description of your content and key words. Think about it as a teaser to your site. For example, an online food magazine may want to include a description such as "Cook with style. 100% plant-based and seasonal recipes available on our online catalogue".

- **Include internal links.**

Adding hyperlinks within your content to other relevant pages on your site can also optimise your engine search results. For example, if your website is explaining how to make a caramelised onion and goats cheese tart, you may want to provide a link to your "Top 10 tips for caramelising onions" page.

There are a number of other strategies which you can deploy for SEO, but these move beyond the scope of creating content. For example, the layout of your website and its visual appeal will highly impact whether a user stays on.

Blog writing

What is blog writing?

A blog is a website that focuses on written content. This can range from lifestyle to news blogs -- key is their personal take. Blogs, then, usually write through a first-person perspective, emphasise personal experiences and include a comments section where they can interact with their readers. This is especially important to its success; having a steady and loyal readership base ensures a consistent flow of user traffic (Chow, 2020).

Now, you may be thinking – how is this related to technical writing? Blogs are quite unusual in the technical writing category due to their uncharacteristic personal style. However, blog writing is an important and widespread style of web writing. As Biggs and White (2011) put it, "blogging at its most basic level is the keeping of an online journal" (p.39). The term comes from the combination of *web* and *log*, or a log of a piece of information online (Biggs & White, 2011).

Anyone can have a blog, but being a blogger takes a lot of dedication and hard work. Keeping a blog alive, with active readers, and innovative content, is considerably difficult. The following section provides useful tips on how to blog successfully.

If you're thinking about starting a blog, you should start by asking yourself what you would like to write about. The main questions to contemplate are:

- What do you know about?
- What are you passionate about?

The more specific your focus is, and the more informed you are on your topic, the easier it will be to target a well-defined audience and appeal to regular readers. It is also useful to research existing blogs on your area of interest. Knowing what is already on the web can help you define what you can bring with your blog.

How to get started

There are many websites for new blog starters, which will host your page on their servers for free. These include WordPress, TumblR, LiveJournal, or Blogger and many others. Using these services is certainly the easiest way to create a blog without having to learn the basics of HTML code. By utilizing these, you also avoid needing to register a domain, and self-host your website. These platforms allow you to choose a theme and customize your blog.

The other important step, intuitively, is to choose a title. Choose something which resonates with you and your readers, and with keywords that search engines can easily pick up (remember SEO!).

Finally, once you're all set up, remember the most important requirement of holding a successful blog: regularity. Posting consistently (Biggs & White, 2011) is the only way to effectively build a faithful reader base with an appetite for more.

Exercises

1. What differentiates blogs from other forms of technical writing?
2. Name five ways to practice SEO.
3. You're writing an online piece on the best things to do in Japan. What are some of the keywords that you might want to include in your article?
4. What is a "meta description" and why is it used?

NOTES

_____

_____

_____

_____

_____

_____

Chapter 11:
How To Use and Interpret Graphics

What are graphics?

The use of graphics is a crucial part of technical documentation (Parker, 2020) -- providing a visual aid to oftentimes bland and lengthy text. This can help to break up your work, reiterate and emphasise a particular point and make complex information more digestible.

The type of graphic that you choose to illustrate your text is highly dependent on the information you wish to convey. For example, if you have written a business plan and want to show your future projections for financial growth, you would probably opt to display this information on a line graph (more on this later). Different types of graphics include:

- Tables
- Charts
- Graphs
- Infographics

How to use graphics?

Though the use of graphics may seem like a basic and straightforward process, there are a number of hidden considerations. Here are a few pointers to bear in mind (Parker, 2020):

Keep it simple. What would be the point in an overly complicated and crowded graphic? Remember that illegible graphics can be very off putting to a reader.

- **Use when necessary.** It may be tempting to highlight every conclusion that you come to with an explanatory diagram, however, this may clutter your work. Central to using graphics is striking an important balance with your text. Only use them when they elevate your piece!
- **Quality is key.** Graphic designs should be clean and visually appealing.
- **Choose your colours wisely.** Does the colour palette of your graphic fit with the rest of your work? What kind of message is this conveying? Too much red on your piece, for example, may send alarm bells to your reader. An overuse of luminous yellow may, similarly, be an eyesore. Think about the overall cohesion of your work.

Tables

Tables are used in technical writing, when presenting categorical information, such as textual or numerical. As one of the simplest forms of graphic, there are not many complications when creating a table. However, there are a few important formatting rules.

Remember that tables are organised in rows and columns, divided by headings, with a title placed at the top or on the first row. Additionally, the far-left column is left aligned whilst the remainder of the table is central.

When constructing a table, remember to (McMurrey, 2020):

- **Prioritize the most important information.** A mammoth 40 column table will probably take up too much space in your work and confuse your reader. Display the information that most closely supports your point.

- **Refer to your table in the text.** It would seem slightly disjointed to include a table without any explanation, especially when it is included to illustrate a point. Providing a short summary of the most important parts of your table will also help your reader's understanding.
- **Don't put measurements in every box.** If you are recording numerical data, such as that organised in dollars, there is no need to put a dollar sign in every box. Include this in the column or row heading.
- **Include footnotes when necessary.** If your table comes from a specific source, or you need to elaborate on a point, put this as a footnote at the bottom.

Example: The following table displays numerical data.

Table 7. Pet population in the U.S. by total number (million) from 2000 to 2020[1]

Year	Cats	Dogs	Rabbits
2000	73	68	5
2010	86	83	6
2020	94	90	8

Source: ThisisanexampleandnotanaccurateestimationoftheUSpetpopulation.com

This does not include "exotic" cats or dogs.

Charts and graphs

The difference between the data included in tables versus charts and graphs is not significant - in fact, you can usually opt for either when choosing a graphic. The main difference, however, is in the precision (McMurrey, 2020). Whilst graphs give a better overall sense of trends, such as in an increasing U.S. cat population over time, they do not provide data in as much detail as a table. You should opt for using charts of graphs, then, when you want to emphasise an observable pattern in your data. Graphs and charts may seem quite daunting, but, really, they are quite simple to use if you have the correct software installed. Many office programmes have easy to understand graph and chart options that can be found in the insert tab.

When formatting a chart of a graph, make sure to include (McMurrey, 2020):

- **Axis labels.** Include these where applicable. What do your y and x axis (or each pie slice) represent? Remember, the y axis is the vertical part of your graph or chart and the x axis is the horizontal section. For example, your x axis may represent years whilst your y axis may indicate total number of pets (in millions).

- **Figure titles.** Place the title of your graph/chart underneath or on top. Make sure to cite the source if this is not original data.

- **Keys.** If you are presenting data from more than one categor then you will need a guide to which bits represent what. On a line graph, for example, a blue line may indicate "cats" and a orange line may indicate "dogs". Include this information in a box situated in an open space on your chart or graph.

- **Information in the text.** As with introducing a table in your work, it is essential that you reference any charts or graphs with more information in your text. Failure to do so may cause some confusion amongst your readers!

There are a number of different graphs and charts that you can draw from. Here are the most commonly used ones (NCES, 2020):

1. **Line graphs** - Line graphs can demonstrate changes over longer and shorter periods of time. They are better to use than bar charts when there are smaller changes that you want to emphasise. They are also useful for comparing changes among different categories (i.e. cats and dogs) over the same amount of time.

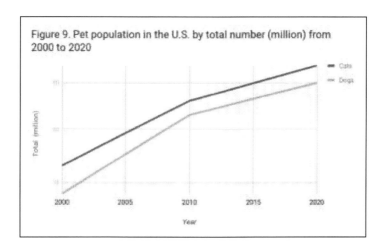

Figure 9. Pet population in the U.S. by total number (million) from 2000 to 2020

2. **Pie charts** - Pie charts do not show changes over time and are best at comparing different parts of a whole. For example, you may wish to show the total distribution of pets (percentage) in the U.S. in the year 2000 with a pie chart.

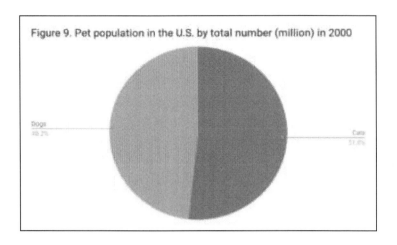

3. **Bar charts** - Like line graphs, bar charts are used to make comparisons between different categories and/or to observe changes over time. Bar charts are better opted for when you want to emphasis large differences between categories.

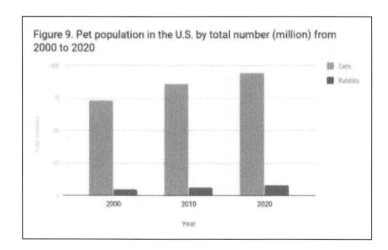

USEFUL LANGUAGE		
Introducing data	The chart shows, the graph displays, the table exhibits, etc....	
Describing Trends	**Key Words**	**Example**
Going up	increase; upward trend; rising; an improvement; a surge; etc...	There is an increase in employment numbers.
Going down	decrease; downward trend; decreasing; a decline; a slump; etc...	There is a decrease in sales for the month of March.
No Change	constant; unchanged; stable; etc...	The grade distributions for the past 6 semesters remain constant.
Frequent Change	fluctuation or fluctuate	The patient's lab results continue to fluctuate.
At the highest point	at the peak; peaking	This year's sales numbers peak in the month of August.
At the lowest point	at its low point; hit the lowest point; at its trough	The current unemployment numbers are at its lowest points since 1979.

Changes (in speed)	quickly, gradually, slowly, etc....	The patient's temperature quickly rose due to an acute infection.
Changes (in degree)	significantly, substantially, dramatically, slightly, a little, slowly, etc...	The student's performance improved dramatically.
Comparison	whereas, in contrast, contrasting, in comparison, comparing, etc...	Whereas my morning class' highest grade was a C, my afternoon class' highest grade was an A+.

Infographics

Infographics are graphic representations of data, knowledge, or information. They can emphasise a particular point and make it more comprehensible. In fact, the use of infographics has been proven to enhance the ability of the human mind to digest information (Segue, 2014).

There are a wide variety of infographic forms to choose from, and hundreds of free templates online - you by no means, however, have to stick to one particular format. Types of infographic include:

- **Geographic infographics.** These are useful when providing information about a specific geographic area, using a map as the key visual. The information included can range from demographic data to top things to do in the area.

- **Timeline infographics.** This is the type of visual used when displaying the history of something, or when highlighting important dates and events. Use aids such as lines and photos to help emphasise your graphic.

- **Statistical infographics.** Detailing data results, survey information, or a specific argument can be a tiresome and waffly enterprise. Arranging these in statistical infographics helps put the emphasis on your findings without the need for long winded jargon. You may wish to include charts and graphs in this type of visual.

- **Informational infographics.** Use informational graphics when you want to elaborate on a concept or provide information on a particular topic. These are often split into distinct sections with headers. Include a number in your title to draw your audience in, such as "10 reasons to visit Oxford".

- **Process infographics.** Think about a standard flow chart - a step by step on a particular topic. This is the best type of infographic to use when providing an overview of a process.

- **Comparison infographics.** Use a comparison infographic to compare two or more items. You may want to split your graphic vertically or horizontally, with key information under your item title.
Hierarchical infographics. When you want to rank information, you can opt for a hierarchical infographic. This could be in the form of a pyramid, with the "most..." at the top and the "least... "at the bottom.

List infographics. These replace standard bullet points lists with visual representations.

Exercises

1. You want to use a chart/graph to display large differences between two categories over time. Which chart/graph is most appropriate and why?
2. Your company has a long history that you want to emphasise in your business plan. What type of graphic would you use to demonstrate this?
3. Detailed financial projections need to be provided in a report. What graphic would you opt for and why?
4. Without checking, what labels need to be included on a standard graph?

NOTES

_____

_____

_____

_____

_____

_____

_____

Conclusion

And that concludes technical writing. What you may have once considered as an intimidating and complicated writing form, you will hopefully now see as something that isn't actually that hard to crack. Whether its writing a job application, sending a memo report at work, or constructing a user manual, this guide has had you covered.

A final note on technical writing: follow the steps and remember your PATs. No matter how difficult something may appear to be, if you break it down and think it through, you will succeed.

References

ACS. (2020, 05 19). *Technical Writing*. Retrieved from ACS Distance Education: https://www.acsedu.co.uk/Info/Publishing/Industry-Training/Technical-Writing.aspx

Anastasia. (2018, January 25). *Basics of Plain Language in Technical Documentation*. Retrieved from ClickHelp: https://clickhelp.com/clickhelp-technical-writing-blog/basics-of-plain-language-in-technical-documentation/

Anderson, A. (2013, Fall). *Writing a Memo Report*. Retrieved from Engineering Union : http://www.engineering.union.edu/~andersoa/WritingaMemo

Ashford University. (2019). *Writing an Executive Summary*. Retrieved from Writing Center: https://writingcenter.ashford.edu/writing-executive-summary

Balmaceda, K. (2018, August 20). *Progress Report: How To Write, Structure And Make It Visually Attractive*. Retrieved from Piktochart: https://piktochart.com/blog/progress-report/

Biggs, J., & White, C. (2012). *Bloggers Boot Camp*. MA, US; Oxford, UK: Focal Press.

Boyd, N. (2020). *How to Write Progress Reports: Purpose, Structure & Content*. Retrieved from Study.com: https://study.com/academy/lesson/how-to-write-progress-reports-purpose-structure-content.html

Busch, S. (2019, April 25). *Should I include a picture in my CV?* Retrieved from Graduateland: https://graduateland.com/article/profile-picture-cv

Chow, S. (2020, May 5). *How To Start A Blog In 2020*. Retrieved from TheBlogStarter: https://www.theblogstarter.com/

ggins, M. (2020). *Business reports*. Retrieved from The University of Melbourne Library : https://library.unimelb.edu.au/__data/assets/pdf_file/0005/1924160/Business_Reports.pdf

noch, D. (2001). Once You Start Using Slippery Slope Arguments, You're on a Very Slippery Slope . *Oxford Journal of Legal Studies 21(4)*, 629–647,.

ExpensePoint. (2020). *The Importance Of Better Expense Reporting*. Retrieved from ExpensePoint: https://www.expensepoint.com/importance-better-expense-reporting/

Faigley, L. (2011). *The Little Penguin Handbook*. Pearson.

Forsey, C. (2020, March 24). *How to Write an Incredibly Well-Written Executive Summary [+ Example]*. Retrieved from Hubspot: https://blog.hubspot.com/marketing/executive-summary-examples

Freshbooks. (2020). *How to Write an Annual Report: 4 Tips for Preparing Annual Reports*. Retrieved from Freshbooks: https://www.freshbooks.com/hub/reports/write-an-annual-report

Glassdoor. (2015, January 20). *50 HR & Recruiting Stats That Make You Think*. Retrieved from Glassdoor for Employers: https://www.glassdoor.com/employers/blog/50-hr-recruiting-stats-make-think/

Gotter, A. (2017, July 5). *The 8 Main Different Types of Content and How to Use Them*. Retrieved from Adespresso : https://adespresso.com/blog/main-different-types-content-use/

Hamlin, A., Rubio, C., & DeSilva, M. (2020). *Communicating Online: Netiquette* . Retrieved from Open Oregon: https://openoregon.pressbooks.pub/technicalwriting/chapter/1-3-netiquette/?fbclid=IwAR2PYFnFjgJpMuoHhuCu6ktu73Lq4MaOjf1i3cnlXZ XSSbdPcrT3WMEOo

Hartwell, D. (2020). *How to Write an Abstract: Brief Steps and Structure Example*. Retrieved from Customwriting.org: https://custom-writing.org/blog/how-to-write-an-abstract

Heathfield, S. (2019, June 12). *What Are Meeting Minutes and Who Records Them at a Meeting?* Retrieved from The Balance Careers: https://www.thebalancecareers.com/what-are-meeting-minutes-and-who-records-them-1918733

Higgs, M. (2019, May 27). *How to Deal With Job-Search Depression*. Retrieved fro New York Times: https://www.nytimes.com/2019/05/27/smarter-living/how-to-deal-with-job-search-depression.html

Indiana University. (2011). *Writing abstracts.* Retrieved from Writing guides: https://wts.indiana.edu/writing-guides/pdf/writing-abstracts.pdf

Jogi, O. (2020). *How to Write a Progress Report* . Retrieved from Weekdone: https://blog.weekdone.com/guide-how-to-write-an-excellent-progress-report-sample-template/

Lanham, R. (2006). *The Economics of Attention: Style and Substance in the Age of Information.* Chicago, IL: University of Chicago Press.

Leroux Miller, K. (2020, March 21). *How to Write an Annual Report for Your Nonprofit.* Retrieved from The balance small business: https://www.thebalancesmb.com/write-nonprofit-annual-report-2502336

Lewinson, M. (2012, December 21). *How to Write a Feasibility Study Report.* Retrieved from Mymanagementguide: https://mymanagementguide.com/feasibility-study-reporting-steps-to-writing-a-feasibility-study-report-fsr/

LSE Careers. (2020). *A guide to CVs, cover letters and application forms.* Retrieved from LSE Careers: https://info.lse.ac.uk/current-students/careers/Assets/Documents/application-and-cv-brochure.pdf

Lumen. (2020). *Executive Summary.* Retrieved from Lumen Planning for Small Business: https://courses.lumenlearning.com/montgomerycollege-planningforsmallbusiness/chapter/executive-summary/

Lumen. (2020). *Purpose, Audience, Tone, and Content.* Retrieved from Lumen Learning: https://courses.lumenlearning.com/ivytech-engl111/chapter/purpose-audience-tone-and-content/

Lumen. (2020). *What is a Feasibility Study/Report.* Retrieved from Lumen Learning - Technical Writing : https://courses.lumenlearning.com/alamo-technicalandbusinesswriting/chapter/unit-4-b_feasibility-report_readings-2/

McGurgan, H. (2020). *What Is the Purpose of Company Annual Reports?* Retrieved from Small Business Chron: https://smallbusiness.chron.com/purpose-company-annual-reports-57428.html

McMurrey, D. (1997). *Tables, Charts, Graphs Show me the data.* Retrieved from Prismnet: https://www.prismnet.com/~hcexres/textbook/tables.html

McMurrey, D. (2020). *Proposals*. Retrieved from PressBooks :
https://coccoer.pressbooks.com/chapter/proposals/

Merloo, J. M. (1967). Contributions of psychiatry to the study of human
communications. In I. F. (Ed.), *Human communication theory: Original
Essays* (pp. 131-159). New York: Holt, Rinehart and Winston.

Mohan, K., & Sharma, R. (2016). *Business Correspondence and Report Writing* .
New Delhi : McGraw Hill Education (India).

Morgan, M. (2020, April 5). *How to Write a Proposal*. Retrieved from WikiHow:
https://www.wikihow.com/Write-a-Proposal

Moz. (2020). *What is SEO?* Retrieved from Moz: https://moz.com/learn/seo/what-
is-seo

Mukhlis, & H. (2015, March 27). *Writing abstracts*. Retrieved from Slideshare:
https://www.slideshare.net/HabibJoelAlMukhlis/week-10-abstracts-2

Myers, A. (2020, April 2&). *4 Tips to Make the Most of Board Meetings*. Retrieved
from Personify: https://personifycorp.com/blog/4-tips-to-make-the-most-
of-board-meetings

Naas, J. (2020). *Know your purpose*. Retrieved from Open Oregon:
https://openoregon.pressbooks.pub/technicalwriting/chapter/x-3-
concept-2-know-your-
purpose/?fbclid=IwAR3uUdgHFtofpHYPgqllOj3Zvv6TXHQ-61fNLJ-
nddzg1v4TSO9SMej2B2g

NCES. (2020). *How to choose which type of graph to use?* Retrieved from Graphing
Tutorial: https://blog.hubspot.com/marketing/executive-summary-
examples

Oliver, V. (2020, March 5). *How To Write Minutes of Meeting Effectively (with
Examples)*. Retrieved from Lifehack:
https://www.lifehack.org/804185/meeting-minutes

Parker, K. (2020, January 2). *Graphics in Technical Writing*. Retrieved from
Medium- Technical Writing is Easy : https://medium.com/technical-
writing-is-easy/graphics-in-technical-writing-1c573441488b

Philosophy, S. E. (2020, April 2). *Fallacies* . Retrieved from Stanford Encyclopedia
Philosophy: https://plato.stanford.edu/entries/fallacies/

ProPapers. (2017, May 24). *How to Write a Short Report?* Retrieved from ProPapers: https://pro-papers.com/blog/write-short-report

Ryan, L. (2015, September 24). *Five Reasons Job-Hunting Is Harder Than It Should Be*. Retrieved from Forbes: https://www.forbes.com/sites/lizryan/2015/09/24/five-reasons-job-hunting-is-harder-than-it-should-be/#2608fa6d2d28

Sherman. (2019, November 8). *What is SEO and How It Works for Small Businesses*. Retrieved from Lyfe Marketing: https://www.lyfemarketing.com/blog/what-is-seo-and-how-it-works/

Smith, J. (2013, April 17). *7 Things You Probably Didn't Know About Your Job Search*. Retrieved from Forbes: https://www.forbes.com/sites/jacquelynsmith/2013/04/17/7-things-you-probably-didnt-know-about-your-job-search/#58ee83653811

Smyth, R. (2004). *The Principles of Writing in Psychology*. London, UK: Red Globe Press.

Sweat, S. (2020). *Summaries & Abstracts in Technical Documents*. Retrieved from Study.com: https://study.com/academy/lesson/summaries-abstracts-in-technical-documents.html

The Segue Creative Team . (2014, April 4). *What Are Infographics and When Should You Use Them?* Retrieved from Segue Technologies: https://www.seguetech.com/infographics/

The University of Oxford Careers . (2019, December 16). *Cover Letters*. Retrieved from The University of Oxford Careers Service: http://www.careers.ox.ac.uk/cover-letters/

United States Census Bureau. (2017, March 30). *Highest Educational Levels Reached by Adults in the U.S. Since 1940*. Retrieved from United States Census Bureau: https://www.census.gov/newsroom/press-releases/2017/cb17-51.html

University Education Committee and Education Board. (2020). *Academic Quality and Policy Office*. Retrieved from University of Bristol: http://www.bristol.ac.uk/academic-quality/groups/edcmtt.html#tor

University of Kansas. (2019, May). *PREWRITING STRATEGIES*. Retrieved from University of Kansas Writing Center: https://writing.ku.edu/prewriting-strategies

University, C. S. (2020). *Citation Guide*. Retrieved from WAC Clearinghouse: https://wac.colostate.edu/resources/writing/guides/apa/

Wallwork, A. (2014). *User Guides, Manuals and Technical Writing: A Guide to Professional English* . New York: Springer.

Walton. (2010). Why Fallacies Appear to Be Better Arguments than They Are. *Informal Logic 30(2)*, 1-21.

Whately, R. (1875). *Elements of Logic.* London: 9th ed. Longmans, Green and Company; first edition 1826.

Yale, C. D. (2020). *Maximizing Your Cover Letter.* Retrieved from Career Development at Yale : https://your.yale.edu/sites/default/files/maximizing_your_coverletter_gu de_2016.pdf

Serena Henning, a Florida native, worked in Human Resources (HR) for a variety of companies over the years. She started out as an office assistant. She then moved on to become a secretary, an office manager, and an executive secretary. She has then moved on to become a consultant for two companies, which includes advising and training in all things involving HR. When she is away from the office, Serena enjoys camping, hiking, and photography. Serena's ultimate camping goal is to camp at Denali National Park in Alaska. This is her first book.

Made in the USA
Middletown, DE
21 December 2020